The Vikings

PAST IMPERFECT

Past Imperfect presents concise critical overviews of the latest research by the world's leading scholars. Subjects cross the full range of fields in the period ca. 400—1500 CE which, in a European context, is known as the Middle Ages. Anyone interested in this period will be enthralled and enlightened by these overviews, written in provocative but accessible language. These affordable paperbacks prove that the era still retains a powerful resonance and impact throughout the world today.

Director and Editor-in-Chief
Simon Forde, *'s-Hertogenbosch*

Production
Ruth Kennedy, *Adelaide*

Cover Design
Martine Maguire-Weltecke, *Dublin*

The Vikings

**Sæbjørg Walaker Nordeide
and Kevin J. Edwards**

British Library Cataloguing in Publication Data

A catalogue record for this book is available from the British Library

ISBN (print): 9781942401896
e-ISBN (PDF): 9781942401902
e-ISBN (EPUB): 9781942401919

www.arc-humanities.org
Printed and bound by CPI Group (UK) Ltd, Croydon, CR0 4YY

Contents

List of Illustrations

Text Boxes

The authors wish to thank the following who have kindly given permission to reproduce illustrations or have assisted in their production:

Figures 1, 6, 12, 15, 18, 20, 22, 23, 27, and 29 were produced by Jamie Bowie of the School of Geosciences, University of Aberdeen.

Figure 2 is after R. I. Page in Viking og Hvidekrist, ed. Else Roesdahl (Copenhagen: Nordisk Ministerråd, 1992), 162. Courtesy Nordisk Ministerråd.

Figures 3, 16, 26, and 31: photographs by S. W. Nordeide.

Figure 4: photograph by Jörg Hempel, and Figure 5, both from Wikimedia Commons.

Figure 7: photographs: top—Harald Faith-Ell, Riksantikvarieämbetet; bottom—one of the chambered graves included what is often discussed as the 'warrior woman' (Bj 581), Evald Hansen based on the original drawing by Hjalmar Stolpe, "Ett och annat på Björkö," Ny illustrerad tidning 25 (1889): 4–16.

Figures 8 and 10: Museum of Cultural History, University of Oslo; Figures 9 and 11: photograph by the University Museum, University of Bergen; Figure 19, photograph: British Museum. All licensed by https://creativecommons.org/licenses/by-sa/4.0/.

Figure 13: drawing by Lars Jørgensen, in The Viking World, ed. Stefan Brink and Neil Price (London: Routledge, 2012). Courtesy S. Brink.

Figure 14: after Bergljot Solberg, Jernalderen i Norge (2003), p. 233. Courtesy Cappelen Akademisk Forlag.

Figure 17: drawing by Michael Hefferman, National Museum of Ireland.

Figures 21, 23, 28, 30, and 32: photographs by K. J. Edwards.

Figure 24: from Church et al. in Quaternary Science Reviews 77 (2013): 228–32.

Figure 25: photograph by David Zori.

Text Box 1: The Viking Ship Museum in Roskilde, Denmark, kindly permitted us to print the excerpts.

Text Box 2: Printed with permission from New York University Press.

Text Box 3: Permission to print provided by The School of Celtic Studies of the Dublin Institute for Advanced Studies.

Preface

"The Vikings" hold a universal fascination which has persisted for centuries. From the horrific tales of Alcuin of York in the eighth century CE/AD and the eleventh-century Adam of Bremen, via the heroic saga literature of Iceland recorded in the thirteenth to fourteenth centuries, through to nineteenth-century Scandinavian romanticism, the Norsemen have engendered fear and occasionally admiration. The appropriation of Viking art and symbolism by the Nazis led to a low point in wider social approval, but in terms of scholarly attention the Vikings have regained their popularity both inside and outside of universities. The Vikings appear frequently in fantasy films and books, they are brought to "life" through re-enactments and music, exhibitions and conferences, attracting thousands of adherents. No wonder—the Viking Age is a dynamic and important part of human history, significant to the foundation of the modern states of Scandinavia and the wider Nordic world, as well as having exerted a major influence on the histories of other countries.

In this concise book, it would be unrealistic to give voice to all aspects, directions, and attitudes concerning Viking research, nor is it possible to extemporize on the popularity of the Vikings. Rather, we address some key issues concerning life, society, economy, and environment during the Viking Age. Study of the Vikings may induce disparate, strong feelings according to whether they are perceived as adventurers or colonisers. We hope that the combination of authors from

Scandinavia and the UK, addressing such dichotomies, will benefit from their varied backgrounds in archaeology and geography, as well as familiarity with Scandinavia, the British Isles, the North Atlantic region, and the associated scholarly traditions. In presenting an overview of the Vikings from conceptual, ideological, and material perspectives, in their homelands and beyond, the approach reflects the interdisciplinary and international character of contemporary Viking studies.

We would like to thank Simon Forde for inviting us to write this book and we are very grateful for his comments, and those of an anonymous referee, on a draft of the manuscript.

Chapter 1

The Vikings

The history of the Vikings may be assembled from many sources—documents, archaeology, place names, environmental evidence, genetics, and more. Written sources, such as the English *Anglo-Saxon Chronicle* record raids by "Norsemen" from near the end of the eighth century CE/AD. Apart from sporadic mentions of such intruders from many sources in the ensuing centuries, the first comprehensive accounts of the Vikings and their activities date primarily after ca. 1200. Given the lateness of such records, they cannot necessarily be considered as totally reliable, although some of the content, including that of the Icelandic sagas, may find apparent confirmation in older documents and subsequent research findings. Archaeological data are time- and place-specific, but they are without words and may be difficult to interpret in terms of their full biographies. Place names often change with time. Environmental sources can be informative regarding landscape impacts and socio-economic activities, while isotopes and genetics may contribute detailed life histories of people, crops, and domesticated animals. Combining all these sources allows a depiction of the history of the Vikings.

Who Were the Vikings?

We may choose to try to explain a number of phenomena during the Viking period, involving concepts such as "Vikings," "Viking Age," and "Scandinavians." These terms are typically associated, but how? Based on Old Norse evidence, it has been argued that "in the Viking Age a Scandinavian was not a Viking simply because he was a Scandinavian."[1] But was he a Scandinavian if he was "a Viking"? And was the Viking only a "he"?

The term Viking was first used in Old English sources, and referred to robbers and coastal marauders.[2] In Scandinavia (taken to refer to Norway, Sweden, and Denmark; Figure 1) the term has its origins in nineteenth-century Sweden.[3] The etymology of the word *viking* is explained in different ways, none of them certain: it may refer to the word *wic* (a camp or trading place), or to the Norse *vik* (a bay).[4] It has been suggested that the word is derived from *vík(j)a*—"move or step aside, turn to the side."[5] This would mean that a rower, when his boat was not under sail, would step aside when tired and his place would be taken by another.

Viking, as a concept, can refer to a person or a group of persons (*víkingr*, pl. *víkingar*), or a kind of activity (*víking*). The meaning may even have changed during the Viking and Middle Ages. For Scandinavia, the Viking Age simply covers a time period, generally cited as ca. 800–1050. During this period, people lived more or less as they had done for centuries, providing for themselves by arable and pastoral agriculture, fishing, and hunting. A few would be specialist crafts-people, and others would sail beyond Scandinavia to raid, conquer, trade, and settle.

Outside Scandinavia, the Vikings are associated with hit-and-run attacks, robbing abbeys and other sacred and secular places. This traditionally began with the raid on the island of Lindisfarne in 793, although this was not the first recorded assault on the British Isles and many other territories were subjected to such violations.[6] Perhaps this was the reason why efforts were made, from Germany and Britain especially, to convert pagan Scandinavians to Christianity in the belief, *inter alia*, that this would result in peace. Amongst others, an archbishopric was founded in Hamburg in 831, and merged with that of Bremen in 845, with the single purpose of providing a bridgehead for the conversion of Scandinavians.

Figure 1. A geographical overview of the Vikings,
Scandinavia, and the Scandinavian diaspora.

Several scholars have argued that the Anglo-Saxon church
contributed even more to this process.[7]

The plundering sea-borne foreigners were often referred
to as "Danes," "Northmen," "heathens," or "pirates," and they
might be mentioned more specifically as coming from Jylland in Denmark or Vestfold and Hordaland in Norway. Even
if information in documentary records provides generalized
information on Vikings and ethnicity in Britain and Ireland,
the specifics remain unclear—to the English, for example, the
marauders would all likely sound the same.[8] In the regions
east of the Baltic Sea, "Northmen" were known under names
such as "Rhos"/"Rus" and "Varangians."[9] In Old Swedish Rus
means *roþs*—originally denoting rower, or seafaring warriors
in rowed ships.[10] This understanding of Rus fits well with the
"rower" interpretation of the word Viking cited earlier. Scandinavians in eastern Europe were probably not culturally uniform, but represented people with the ability to assimilate
and to adapt culturally.[11] Arabic sources reported the Rus as
being merchants as well as raiders.[12]

Conspicuous wealth is to be found in the Norwegian ship
graves at Oseberg and Gokstad from the 800s onwards and
also in earlier boat-graves at Vendel and Valsgärde in Swe-

den. Only the elite would be despatched in this manner. Archaeological and written sources indicate the role of ships in overseas raiding expeditions, and they were, of course, vital for carrying goods as part of everyday commerce.

In this book "Vikings" will be discussed in terms of the (mainly) Old Norse-speaking regions of Scandinavia, and emigrants from the same area, in the Viking Age. Scandinavians here are considered as including raiders, adventurers, and merchants as well as exiles and those travelling outside Scandinavia to establish permanent settlement, or eventually returning to their homeland. In addition, there may have been many and varied motivations behind their travels. This would include most of the groups under names like Rus, Varangians, and Northmen in Eastern Europe, and Danes, pirates, Northmen, and heathens in southern and western Europe. When it comes to the Viking diaspora into what were essentially unsettled areas, especially the North Atlantic islands beyond Britain, the term "Norse" is commonly applied.

When Was the Viking Age?

Typically, the Viking Age is dated to ca. 800–1050 in Scandinavia. As already mentioned, the traditional start of the period is cited as the first attacks on the geographical area of the British Isles, although Scandinavian military expeditions started earlier than the Lindisfarne attack of 793; among others to Portsmouth in 789 and probably prior to this. Depending on the criteria applied, there can be considerable variation to the date range. A recently suggested start around 700 is based on the fact that the earliest Scandinavian trading centre of Ribe was founded in the early eighth century, including apparent contacts between Scandinavia and the British Isles.[13]

The end-date is also a movable feast. In Scandinavia, it can depend on such criteria as Christianization, urbanization, state formation, the occurrence of written sources, typology, or various combinations of these. The date of these events differed geographically, and the chronology of archaeological material as well as documentary evidence may often be questionable. It is not usually possible to date an archaeological site precisely, and information in late, written sources often presents serious interpretational problems. For Norway, some authors would use the year 1030 as the year of conversion (the year when Olav, the patron saint, was killed in a battle at Stiklestad), even if non-Christian graves are evident until the end of the eleventh century. Some would argue that the Viking Age ended when the last Danish king of England, Cnut the Great (Canute), died in 1035, or when "the last Viking king," King Haraldr Hardráði from Norway, was killed at the Battle of Stamford Bridge in 1066.

New finds represent a problem for the chronology. Traditional timespans are mostly pinned to events testified in written sources, all based on British–Scandinavian connections and which pay scant attention to other areas. If Vikings are to be defined as groups of raiders originating in Scandinavia, then archaeological sources suggest that initial activity spread eastwards from Sweden, and not westwards to Britain and Ireland. Reference has already been made to rich boat-graves at Vendel and Valsgärde. At Varlsgärde five graves from the seventh and the eighth centuries and ten from the ninth to the mid-eleventh century included similar finds, with all fifteen boat-graves containing males only and an extraordinarily rich suite of grave goods.[14] Excavations on the opposite side of the Baltic at Salme, Estonia, revealed two ships, loaded with armed men from the period 650–780.[15] These men may well have come from eastern Sweden and were prevented from making the journey home. At least for the ninth and tenth centuries there is a neat correspondence between archaeological and documentary (particularly Arabic) sources regarding activity to the east, demonstrating the existence of Scandinavian arrivals associated with the name Rus.[16] Scandinavians travelled by boat along major rivers such as the Volga, and bodies of water such as the Caspian and Black Seas, all the way to Turkey. Albeit a potentially ambiguous term, "The Rus" are taken here to refer to Scandinavian Viking Age migrants to the east, and representing an important link between Scandinavian, Turkish, and Arabic peoples.

The boat-graves from eastern Sweden and Estonia indicate that Viking activity had started in the seventh or eighth century. But given that earlier sources are so scarce or lack critical study, this book will focus mostly upon the traditional period, from the late eighth until the early to middle years of the eleventh centuries. Such fluidity enables us to make broad temporal comparisons where necessary.

Where Are the Vikings to be Traced?

Scandinavia may be regarded as the homeland of the Vikings, but people from this core area also applied their nautical skills to explorations of the external world. A chieftain from the north of Norway, Ottar (Óttarr/Ohthere) of Hålogaland, told King Alfred of England around the year 890 that he lived furthest to the north of Norse farmers in what he termed "Norðmanna land" or "Norðweg," and he travelled eastwards by going even further to the north and following the coast around the mainland of what is present-day Norway (Text Box 1). The source does not provide a very precise location for Ottar's farm, but the approximate position combined with archaeological sources locates it somewhere north of Lofoten. The area north of this, and the adjacent inland parts of Norway, Sweden, and Finland was the land of the Finns. This territory would be populated by Sámi-speaking peoples who were being taxed by Ottar.[17] The rest of Scandinavia would be the homeland of the Vikings.

Outside Scandinavia, Vikings are to be traced in all directions, although they were not equally distributed. This diaspora (Greek *dia*, "across" + *sperein*, "to scatter") is pertinent to the study of colonization and the process of hybridity between local and non-local populations.[18] Judith Jesch uses the concept "Viking diaspora" as an expression which embraces all locations where Vikings settled outside Scandinavia in a certain period of time. She suggests that such migration areas are characterized by the use of what would now be termed the Old Norse language, together with an associated ethnicity and culture.[19] Apart from sharing a mutual linguistic intelligibility and history, the Vikings would share some characteristics of materiality too. Ethnicity occurs when cultural differences are made relevant through interaction, and cultural differences become particularly apparent at boundaries where encounters with other cultures are experienced. Sharing the same language and immigration history would be important ethnic identifiers. With regard to the Vikings, it is worth noting that cultural identity is a major issue among migrant populations.[20] It would be expected that the view of the Vikings held by non-Scandinavians in the diaspora would differ from the Vikings' view of themselves. Their compatriots in the Viking homelands may have admired or appreciated the wealth and opportunity created by their "own"; whereas, at best, their "otherness" would likely disturb those amongst whom they settled in the diaspora, and at worst, they would have been feared as criminal and cruel usurpers. The migrants were probably not fully representative of Scandinavia as a population—males, for instance, were more likely to migrate than females and children. Of course, Scandinavia was only superficially homogeneous. The region was populated by diverse Sámi- and Norse-speaking groups, with varied agricultural, fishing, and hunting economies and cultures.[21]

To the west of Scandinavia, the existence of Scandinavian migrants is well attested both in documentary and archaeological sources. Place names and archaeology show them to have been present in many parts of the British Isles, especially in the western and northern isles of Scotland, the Danelaw area of England, south Wales, the Isle of Man, and coastal Ireland. Urban centres and monarchies were established in these polities. Presumably as a consequence of over-riding Scandinavian influence, these areas were later included in the archbishopric of Nidaros (present-day Trondheim), founded in 1153, and some of the islands came under the purview of the king of Norway.

The Vikings also settled on the islands further into the North Atlantic. The Faroes were colonized from about 800,

Iceland from around 870, Greenland from 985, and even Newfoundland, briefly, around 1000. This is explored in Chapter 3 but, suffice to say, the archaeological evidence for numerous farmsteads in most of these areas is supported by a large amount of documentary, saga, linguistic, environmental, and genetic data.

There is plentiful evidence, both archaeological and written, for Scandinavians travelling eastwards. Finds of Scandinavian origin are known from the Kiev region at Dnjepr, Volga, Ladoga and in the town of Novgorod (Old Norse: *Holmgarðr*). Waterways were important routes between Scandinavia and Byzantium, and Scandinavians can be traced archaeologically all the way to the Caspian Sea. Occurrences of Scandinavian finds in the Balkans, though, are sparse and include a few finds of weapons dating from the second half of the tenth century and the start of the eleventh.[22]

The name Normandy comes from the word "northmen," which signals a significant presence of "men from the north."[23] It may be assumed that most of them were Scandinavians, or perhaps Norse from the Viking diaspora. The *Royal Frankish Annals* report incursions from "Nordmanni" (Danes) in 777, with repeated attacks, particularly during the ninth century, until eventually the Franks managed to improve their defensive systems. The Norsemen followed rivers inland to Paris and indulged potentially in looting; the Frisian coast too was particularly vulnerable.[24] Latin and Arabic sources report Viking expeditions to the Iberian Peninsula, with many raids in the middle of the ninth century and during the second half of the tenth century. However, the written sources are unreliable, and archaeological sources are generally lacking.[25]

Although Scandinavian ships made it all the way to the eastern parts of the Mediterranean Sea, they left few traces along the shores of North Africa or other areas. Consequently, this is not regarded as part of the "Viking diaspora." The Vikings clearly preferred to travel east by following the waterways via the Baltic Sea and thence continuing east and south by river.

* * *

The Vikings have now been introduced, geographically, chronologically and terminologically. Their name is more or less equivalent to Scandinavians (and hence maps onto Scandinavia). They were known by different names in various parts of Europe and, as dealt with here, the Vikings were certainly operating in the period ca. 800–1050, although the acts of travelling, attacking, and settling had begun earlier. It would seem difficult to produce a definition of "Viking" which fits everywhere for the whole period of time and this stricture is not considered critical to this account.

The geographical area under consideration is therefore extensive and the sources complex. It is not possible to allocate equal weight to all areas and topics. We anticipate that the increasing availability of Viking-related research from eastern Europe[26] and scientific studies in all regions will prove especially significant for future study.

Text Box 1: Ottar's voyage

Ohthere said to his lord, King Alfred, that he lived furthest north of all Northmen [Norwegians]. He said that he lived in the northern part of the land, beside the West Sea. He said however that the land extends a very long way north from there, but it is all waste, except that in a few places here and there *Finnas* camp, engaged in hunting in winter and in summer in fishing by the sea. He said that on a certain occasion he wished to investigate how far the land extended in a northerly direction, or whether anyone lived to the north of the wilderness.

He chiefly went there, in addition to the surveying of the land, for the walruses, because they have very fine bone in their teeth—they brought some of the teeth to the king—and their hide is very good for ships' ropes.

This whale is much smaller than other whales—it is not longer than seven ells long—but the best whale hunting is in his own land: they are forty-eight ells long and the biggest fifty ells long; he said that he and six others killed sixty of them in two days.

He was a very prosperous man in respect of those possessions that their wealth consists of, that is, of wild animals. When he sought the king, he still had six hundred domesticated animals unsold. These animals they call reindeer; six of them were *stæl* reindeer. They are prized among the *Finnas*, since they catch the wild reindeer with them.

He was among the foremost men in that land. However, he did not have more than twenty head of cattle and twenty sheep and twenty pigs, and the little that he ploughed he ploughed with horses. But their wealth consists mostly of the tax that the *Finnas* pay them. The tax consists of animals skins and of bird feathers and whale bone and of those ships' ropes that are made from whale [or walrus?] hide and of seals. Each pays according to his rank [or lineage]: the highest in rank has to pay fifteen marten skins and five reindeer and one bear skin and ten *ambers* of feathers and a bear- or otter-skin tunic and two ships' ropes; each must be sixty ells long, one must be made from whale [or walrus?] hide, the other from sealskin.

Adapted from *Ohthere's Voyages*, ed. Janet Bately and Anton Englert, Maritime Culture of the North 1 (Roskilde: Viking Ship Museum, 2007), 44–46.

Notes

[1] John Lind, "'Vikings' and the Viking Age," in *Stanzas of Friendship: Studies in Honour of Tatjana N. Jackson*, ed. Natalja Yu. Gvozdetskaja et al. (Moscow: Moskva Dmitriy Pozharskiy University, 2011), 7.

[2] Julian D. Richards, *The Vikings. A Very Short Introduction, Very Short Introductions* 137 (Oxford: Oxford University Press, 2005), 3–4.

[3] Joonas Ahola and Frog, eds., *Fibula, Fabula, Fact: The Viking Age in Finland*, Studia Fennica. Historica 18 (Helsinki: Finnish Literature Society, 2014), 23.

[4] Lind, "'Vikings' and the Viking Age."

[5] Eldar Heide, "Víking—'Rower Shifting'? An Etymological Contribution," *Arkiv för nordisk filologi* 120 (2005): 41–54.

[6] Julian D. Richards, *Viking Age England* (Stroud: History Press, 2012), 27–30.

[7] Lesley Abrams, "The Anglo-Saxons and the Christianization of Scandinavia," *Anglo-Saxon England* 24 (1995): 213–49; Olav Tveito, *Ad Fines Orbis Terrae—Like Til Jordens Ender. En Studie i Primær Trosformidling i Nordisk Kristningskontekst*, *Acta Humaniora* 209 (Oslo: Det historisk filosofiske fakultet, Universitetet i Oslo, 2005), 32–70.

[8] Richards, *Viking Age England*, 14.

[9] Fedir Androshchuk, *Vikings in the East: Essays on Contact Along the Road to Byzantium (800–1100)*, Studia Byzantina Upsaliensia 14 (Uppsala: Uppsala Universitet, 2013), 2; Andrzej Buko, ed., *Bodzia: A Late Viking-Age Elite Cemetery in Central Poland*, East Central and Eastern Europe in the Middle Ages, 450–1450 (Leiden: Brill, 2015), 1.

[10] Wladyslaw Duczko, *Viking Rus. Studies on the Presence of Scandinavians in Eastern Europe*, The Northern World 12 (Leiden: Brill, 2004), 23.

[11] Thorir Jonsson Hraundal, "New Perspectives on Eastern Vikings/Rus in Arabic Sources," *Viking and Medieval Scandinavia* 10 (2014): 65–97.

[12] Ann Christys, *Vikings in the South: Voyages to Iberia and the Mediterranean*, Studies in Early Medieval History (London: Bloomsbury, 2015). Peter B. Golden, "Rus," in *Encyclopedia of Islam*, edited by C. E. Bosworth, E. v. Donzel, W. P. Heinrichs, and G. Lecomte. (Leiden: Brill, 1995), 618–29.

[13] Judith Jesch, *The Viking Diaspora*, The Medieval World (London: Routledge, 2015), 8.

14 Birgitta Hårdh, *Grunddragen i Norden Förhistoria* (Lund: University of Lund, Institute of Archaeology, 1993), 134–35.

15 Marge Konsa, Raili Allmäe, and Liina Maldre, "Rescue Excavations of a Vendel Era Boat-Grave in Salme, Saaremaa," *Archaeological Fieldwork in Estonia* for 2008 (2008): 53–64; Jüri Peets et al., "Research Results of the Salme Ship Burials in 2011–2012," *Archaeological Fieldwork in Estonia* for 2012 (2012): 43–60.

16 Thorir Jonsson Hraundal, "The Rus in Arabic Sources: Cultural Contacts and Identity" (PhD diss., University of Bergen, 2013), 33.

17 Håvard Dahl Bratrein, "Ottar," *Norsk biografisk leksikon*, online version at https://nbl.snl.no/Ottar; upload dated February 13, 2009.

18 Ian Lilley, "Diaspora and Identity in Archaeology: Moving Beyond the Black Atlantic," in *A Companion to Social Archaeology*, ed. Lynn Meskell and Robert W. Preucel (Malden: Blackwell, 2004): 287–312.

19 Jesch, *The Viking Diaspora*, 3–5.

20 Thomas Hylland Eriksen, *Small Places, Large Issues: An Introduction to Social and Cultural Anthropology*, 3rd ed. (New York: Pluto, 2010), 275–288 and 319.

21 Fredrik Svanberg, *Decolonizing the Viking Age*, 2 vols., Acta Archaeologica Lundensia 24 and 43 (Lund: Almqvist & Wiksell International, 2003); Jørgen Jensen, *Danmarks Oldtid* (Copenhagen: Gyldendal, 2004), 289–331; Lars Ivar Hansen and Bjørnar Olsen, *Samenes historie: fram til 1750* (Oslo: Cappelen, 2004).

22 Valeri Yotov, "Traces of the Presence of Scandinavian Warriors in the Balkans," in *Byzantium and the Viking World*, ed. Fedir Androshchuk et al. (Uppsala: Uppsala University, 2016), 241–53.

23 Jesch, *The Viking Diaspora*, 27.

24 Janet L. Nelson, "The Frankish Empire," in *The Oxford Illustrated History of the Vikings*, ed. Peter Sawyer (Oxford: Oxford University Press, 1997), 19–47.

25 Christys, *Vikings in the South*, 2–6.

26 Marika Mägi, *The Viking Eastern Baltic* (Leeds: Arc Humanities Press, forthcoming).

Chapter 2

Viking Age Scandinavia

Scandinavia was composed of an amalgam of peoples in
the Viking Age, but depictions of the period tend to make
the population appear more uniform than it was in reality—
part of the process of creating a national history of modern
Sweden, Norway, and Denmark. Even so, if individuals living
outside Scandinavia had inter-married or otherwise become
entwined with people of non-Norse ethnicities, they themselves might well have still identified with Scandinavia, particularly if Old Norse was their principal language. It thus
seems appropriate for a study of the Vikings to take Scandinavia as a starting point.

Sources of Viking Scandinavia are poorer than are found
in contemporary Christian Europe. The Latin alphabet was
introduced by the Church in Scandinavia, and although written sources suggest that missionaries arrived earlier, Christianity was not established formally until towards the end of the
Viking Age, that is the late tenth and early eleventh century.
Christianity began earlier in Denmark than in other Scandinavian countries, starting with the social elite. Even at that, few
people became Christian, and non-Christian, illiterate groups
persisted in various parts of Scandinavia.[27] During most of
the Viking Age, writing in Scandinavia consisted mainly of
simple, short inscriptions (runes) on stone, bone, or wood and
literacy was of a low order. The runic alphabet changed from
twenty-four runes in the early Iron Age to sixteen runes (the
so-called younger *futhark* [= alphabet]) in the late Iron Age,

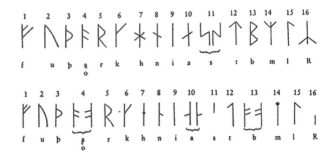

Figure 2. Two main variations of the
Viking Age runic alphabet.

including the Viking Age. The order of runes was consistent,
but there was a greater variation of forms in the Viking Age.
The reduction in the number of runes also reduced their precision because individual runes could have several meanings.
A formulation such as "X erected this stone after Y" is typical.
Uppland in Sweden has more than one thousand rune stones,
often decorated, and displaying a similar format (Figure 2).[28]

Economy and Settlement

The Viking Age economy of Scandinavia was a mixture of
arable agriculture, animal husbandry, fishing, and hunting,
along with the gathering of terrestrial and marine resources.
Of critical importance to Scandinavia, as in northern lands
elsewhere, was the need to acquire winter fodder for the
over-wintering of domesticated animals. Fodder in the form
of pasture and meadow grass, cereal crop residues, and
heathland plants, was stored as feed for sheep, goats, cattle, horses, and pigs. Where available, leaves and twigs were
used to supplement animal foodstuffs.

Wildlife products like falcons and furs from extensive forest and alpine areas were attractive objects for trade, tax
collection, and prestigious gifts. Antler, skins, bog ore, and
stone were important resources for craftsmen and traders.

Whetstones and steatite vessels were among the items circulated within, and exported from, Scandinavia to countries around the North Sea as well as in the North Atlantic region.

Marine resources have always been important to Scandinavia, providing reliable food supplies as well as oil for lighting, sealskin for clothing, whalebone for construction, and, in coastal areas, salt for curation. In addition, walrus ivory was a valuable commodity.[29] Seasonal, specialized fishing communities are recorded along the west coast of Norway, indicating at least partially commercial fisheries. These settlements were possibly exporting to Christian communities in Europe, in need of fish for Lent, before Christianity was established in Scandinavia. Boat houses and landing-places for boats are found in a number of coastal locations.[30]

Seasonality clearly characterized activities such as hunting and the use of summer pastures (shielings, Old Norse *setr*, in a 'transhumance' system). It is likely that the production of iron (from bog iron) and quarrying (e.g., for querns, whetstones, and soapstone) was carried out in the summer months when snow was not a hindrance. Iron as the raw material for many tools and weapons was central to the phenomenon of the "Vikings." Seasonal (and other) activities were probably heavily gendered, with ironworking and metal craftwork by men, textile manufacture and transhumance the domain of women. Even warfare, assuming it was overwhelmingly a masculine enterprise, would have been a seasonal event.

In northern regions it is possible that the Sámi people were domesticating reindeer in the Viking Age, although intensive herding may not have started until the seventeenth century.[31] In parts of southern Scandinavia, agriculture and animal husbandry were more important. Cattle, sheep, and goats were common domesticates, and horses and dogs were kept. Cereals were cultivated, and other wild and domesticated plants (e.g., angelica, hazel, blueberries, raspberries, and apples) were valued for their produce. Place names indicate wild locations for angelica (Norse *kvann*), as in Kvanne and Kvanndal, reflecting the probable importance of the plant. Fishing and hunting were undoubtedly practised in all areas.

Rural settlement was dominated by single farmsteads, but the lay-out of farms and villages varied in different landscapes. In Denmark, with its lack of topographic variation, villages could be large with farms typically of 3,600 to 15,000 square metres in size, increasing through the Viking Age to as much as four hectares (40,000 m²) or ten acres.[32] In other parts of Scandinavia, the diverse topography affected the structure and organization of farmsteads and villages. For instance, although the field systems usually took the form of an intensively used and enclosed "infield" (homefield), including cultivation, and an extensively grazed "outfield," some were markedly irregular in structure if not in functional organization.

Architecture is to some extent consequent upon the nature of the landscape. Other than for Denmark and southern parts of Sweden, rocks and mountains, low temperatures, poor soils, and woodland dominate the Scandinavian land mass. In some regions of Sweden and Norway much stone was used in house construction and this enhances the visible survival of settlement evidence, especially where subsequent landscape utilization was not heavy. In areas of pine and spruce forest, cob houses were built using horizontally-laid timbers. Unfortunately, these wooden constructions are not easily traced as wood is rarely preserved in the dry locations in which people would have chosen to live. Cob houses lack vertical posts which would otherwise produce post holes, and hence such Viking Age wooden houses are strongly under-represented. In Denmark, vertical timbers were often used in construction and post holes survive from numerous settlements, including Tissø and Vorbasse. The posts may be combined with wattle and daub walls.[33] Pit-houses, usually interpreted as workshops and particularly used for textile production, are also found (Figure 3). Although variable, they consisted of small semi-subterranean structures. Their sunken floors were excavated perhaps half a metre below the ground surface, with sub-rectangular floor plans and dimensions of around

Figure 3. Pit house under excavation from Bjørkum in Lærdal, Sogn og Fjordane, Norway.

three by three metres. There are sites where hundreds of pit-houses existed in southern Scandinavia; it is estimated that there were two to three hundred such structures at Tissø. One or two pit-houses may be found on a Viking Age farm[34] and they were also frequent in some of the Viking Age towns like Hedeby and Ribe.[35] For some places, pit-houses may be interpreted as temporary accommodation associated with assembly sites.[36]

Boathouses had an open gable towards the sea, allowing the boat to be hauled ashore. Given the existence of hearths and other debris within boathouses, they would seem to have been occupied intermittently. It is assumed that people could also live temporarily in or under their beached boats during long coastal voyages.

Figure 4. A reconstructed Norse longhouse at
Borg, Lofoten, Norway.

The longhouse—long rather than squat—was the archetypal dwelling type in Viking Age Scandinavia. There was no standard length for a longhouse, but five to fifty metres was not uncommon (see below). It consisted of a three-aisled construction with curved outer walls. Pairs of posts supported the roof and there were often lateral room divisions. The longhouses, which varied in complexity, could provide a home for animals in winter as well as people all year round. The residential part of the house would normally include a central fireplace (hearth) along the main axis of the room, providing heat and light for the people seated or lying on wall benches. The construction of longhouse walls varied greatly and could include any combination of wood, stone, turf (peat), or wattle and daub.

The longest house found, perhaps surprisingly, is at Borg in Lofoten in the far north of Norway, distant from the traditionally richer south. This house was actually built in the eighth century and was rebuilt several times over the following centuries. It was eighty metres long, up to nine metres wide, divided into five areas and with a total area of 600–720 m² (Figure 4).[37] Borg is regarded as having been a chieftain's farm with several additional buildings. Given the rich wildlife resources of northern Norway, attested by Ottar to King Alfred (see Text Box 1 above), then the magnificence of Borg should not be totally unexpected.

Viking settlements were sometimes fortified with earthworks or wooden palisades, as around Birka and Hedeby; concrete or bricks were unknown. The *Danevirke* defensive wall and a series of ring fortresses are certainly impressive. The fortresses were constructed at strategic places around Denmark by King Harald Blåtand (Bluetooth) during the years around 959–987 (e.g., Borgeby and Trelleborg in Skåne, Aggersborg and Fyrkat in Jylland, Nonnebakken in Fyn, Trelleborg and Borgring in Sjælland). It has been suggested that a lost place name in Oslo, Trælaborg/Trælaberg, could indicate Danish ambitions for fortifications there, and parts of a circular fortification in Trondheim from the late tenth century is proposed as a similar edifice. These ring fortresses were a response to a military crisis and intended to defend against external enemies; they represented a colossal input of resources. They were not only inhabited by soldiers, but also by women, children and probably slaves and servants. Isotope analyses of the cemetery at Trelleborg suggest that around thirty-two of forty-eight individuals were born outside southern Scandinavia and perhaps in Norway or central and northern Sweden, or even in Slavic areas. Artisans produced fine and specialized items and it has been surmized that inhabitants were often relatively wealthy, even aristocratic (Figure 5).[38]

Longhouse construction changed from three- to one-aisled during the Viking Age, and earlier than this even at Öland and Gotland in eastern Sweden. Roof-supporting posts also moved to the outer walls, releasing more space inside houses.[39] This type of structure is also seen in the ring fortresses. The longhouse format was exported throughout the Viking world, including across the North Atlantic territories.

Place Names

Place names are important identifiers of Old Norse settlement and activities. They are located in the landscape where people who named the land lived, and where archaeological sources can add to the information.

Figure 5. Aerial photo-
graph of Trelleborg, one
of the ring fortresses
in Denmark.

Many place names used in the Viking Age have been identified, such as names with suffixes like *-staðir*, *-bý*, *-bø*, *-land*,
-säter/-set, although some of them may have been applied
in earlier times.[40] Names tend to cluster in some regions,
revealing organizational structure, as in a *bygd* (a small
settlement district), with cultic and judicial foci on different
places within such an area. In Sweden particularly, but also in
Denmark and Norway, "Central Place Complexes" have been
characterized.[41] These consist of a collection of places with
a representative set of settlement types denoted by names
such as *tuna* or *husa* (a chieftain's farm), *husaby* (sometimes
a royal property), names indicating worship (like Torsåker,
Ullevi, Fröslunda), other names denoting ritual sites (e.g., Vi,
Hov/Hof, Vang, Åker), and compound names indicating places
where warriors stayed, such as Karlaby or Tegneby.[42]

Some farm names are dated earlier than the Viking Age,
but these have survived in various forms up to the present.
In Norway this would include names with suffixes such as
-heim (dwelling, settlement) and *-vin* (meadow). Later names,

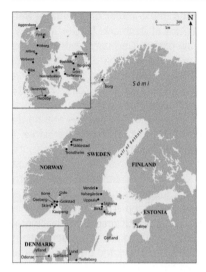

Figure 6. A map of
Scandinavia with
Viking Age towns.

like -*staðir*, tend to occupy a more peripheral location as the
best land was already taken when the places to which these
names were attached became established. Names are not
uniformly distributed: -*land* names are particularly frequent
in Vest-Agder, -*setr* names in Møre, and -*vin* in eastern Norway, Trøndelag, Voss, and Hardanger.[43]

Theophoric names, that is those combined with the name
of a divinity, shows that the worship of specific gods was not
evenly spread in Scandinavia. Place names with Týr are only
found in Denmark, while Freyr and Ullr/Ullin names are concentrated in the southern parts of Norway and Sweden.[44]

Towns and Trade

The first towns or marketplaces of some significance emerged
in Scandinavia from the eighth century. They would seem to
have been well organized settlements, with trade and craft
production as major functions and numerous Viking burials
are found around them (Figure 6).

Some of the first and most important centres were located in the former territory of Denmark. The fortified town of Hedeby (Haithabu, now part of Germany's northernmost state of Schleswig-Holstein), was strategically located on the southern border of Scandinavia from early in the eighth century. Excavation finds and documentary sources prove that it was populated by a mix of Danes, Saxons, and Slavs. There may have been as many as ten thousand graves around the town.[45] The fortifications were linked to the *Danevirke*, a defensive wall of some antiquity securing Denmark's southern border. Ribe, also in southern Denmark, emerged around 700. At the beginning of the ninth century, a two-metre wide ditch, interpreted as a judicial border, was constructed around the town. This ditch was replaced by a fortification during the tenth century. The production of combs, metalwork, and glass beads (although the glass was produced outside Scandinavia) is recorded in Ribe. Land ownership within both Ribe and Hedeby was based on linear plots.[46]

Recent excavations have revealed important information about Ribe. A circular Christian cemetery containing between two and three thousand graves was established there during the ninth century. This may have been associated with the documented church of bishop Ansgar, which may have been constructed initially to attract and function for foreign Christian merchants and craftsmen who would have difficulties staying somewhere without a place of worship. Ribe's location, situated close to the border between Christian and non-Christian territory, may support this idea. The cemetery was initially established outside the earliest (non-Christian) settlement, on the opposite bank of the river. With urban growth, the location was to become central and the cemetery, associated with the later cathedral, has been active ever since.[47]

Birka, located on the island of Björkö, thirty kilometres west of modern Stockholm, was the most significant early marketplace in Sweden. The town was fortified from the ninth century at least, with defensive systems including a town rampart, an underwater palisade and a hill fort. Approximately

Figure 7. View of the grave field beside the Viking emporium, Birka, Sweden (top), and one of the chamber graves at the grave field with the so-called warrior woman (bottom).

two thousand burial mounds and many unmarked inhumation graves are recorded around the island (Figure 7). The settlement was active from the mid-eighth century until about 970. Sigtuna took over the role of Birka as a long-distance trade centre, founded ca. 980.[48] Kaupang, close to Larvik in Oslofjord, was the only town established in Norway in the early Viking Age, existing in the period ca. 800–930 when the region may have been part of the Danish polity. The port at Kaupang was dominated by its island- and land-based burial grounds, with perhaps close to a thousand graves. The sight of the burial mounds would be the first impression of Kaupang gained by visitors. Unlike Birka and Hedeby, Kaupang was not fortified, but like the others it seems to have featured a planned lay-out, a criterion interpreted as reflecting royal initiative.[49]

Towns, of course, did not spring up spontaneously with no purpose beyond housing and the centralization of religion. Trade and its safe facilitation in the Viking Age economy was a key part of the urbanization process. The possibility of concentrating the transfer of goods between customers within a market would have attracted craftspeople and the rise of merchants. The focus of such activity in ports eased the transport of goods both locally and to distant locations within trading networks. Scandinavia was well placed for this, with access to the west (e.g., the North Sea, North Atlantic, and the Mediterranean) and the east (Russia, central Europe, the Black Sea). Local trade would have included such agricultural produce as crops and animals, combs, hones, soap stone products, glass beads, textiles, and farm tools. Some of this was valued by foreign merchants and could be part of the exchange process. Long distant trade would also have involved merchandise such as silver, spices, glass, jewellery, furs, bone, fish, and slaves.

Barter was probably the most common type of trade in the Viking Age. Precious metals, in particular hack silver, were both a frequent commodity and used as money. Gifting was of significant social and political importance, especially for the aristocracy, among whom prestige items such as falcons and ivory were exchanged. This particular activity should be regarded perhaps as a means of cementing bonds of friendship and alliance rather than trade.

Coins were not produced in Scandinavia during most of the Viking Age, and the function of the earliest coins, as imported objects, is debatable—were they keepsakes, heirlooms, or used as money in trade? The occurrence of anonymous *sceattas* in Ribe from the early eighth century have been posited as local or Frisian.[50] Except for these, the earliest minting in Scandinavia may have been started by Danes in Hedeby in the first half of the ninth century, with intermittent production through to the second half of the tenth century under King Harald Bluetooth and King Svend Forkbeard. It is notable that more or less continuous minting was found in all three Scandinavian countries at the same time, in the middle of the 990s. King Svend Forbeard's mint in Denmark and King Olav Tryggvason's coin making in Norway began in 995–1000. The first mint in Sweden was instigated by King Olof Skötkonung in Sigtuna in the middle of the 990s, but production only began consistently around 1100.[51] Although the Swedish and Danish kings also copied Byzantine coins, most Scandinavian coins replicated Anglo-Saxon coins initially, and the same Anglo-Saxon moneyer, Godwine, may have been active in all three countries. Before these instances, a number of foreign coins, particularly Arabic coins (silver and gold dinars and dirhams), were imported and most finds are found in graves.

Writing and calculation, as well as size and weight measurements, were vital to commerce. Balances and weights were used in metal production and most likely in trade. Literacy must have been a weak point however. From the start of the Viking Age the runic alphabet existed. Signs for numbers though are unknown, and calculations must have been difficult, although tally sticks may have been used. These appear regularly in medieval towns in Scandinavia, but even if they occur in the Viking period in the Faroe Islands, for example at Toftanes, it is difficult to find examples from Viking Age Scandinavia.[52] How did people keep track of volumes and numbers of goods, particularly if merchandise was transported?

It appears that some of the earlier Viking Age towns were moved from their places of foundation and re-established as Christian centres at the end of the tenth century. This was perhaps a spiritual distancing from pagan territory—it was noted above that a church site at Ribe was established on the other side of its river, and Birka moved to Sigtuna—but other forces could have been involved. Kaupang may have been abandoned when the Danish king lost his power in this region, or the town possibly moved to Skien where an early church site is recorded. It should not be forgotten that changes in relative sea-level, and a move towards larger ships, necessitated the re-location and reconfiguration of some harbours in order to access deeper waters; Hedeby consequently moved to Schleswig.

At the turn of the millennium, a new series of towns emerged in Scandinavia, of a different character: Trondheim and Oslo in Norway; Lund, Roskilde, and Viborg in Denmark; Sigtuna in Sweden. Some of the earliest Christian sites are to be found in these second-generation towns (e.g., Oslo, Lund, and Ribe), and these may have served their wider regions.[53] The major difference from the earlier urban places is that these new towns seem to have been Christian from the start, and they were likely royal foundations too. A link between urbanization, the Church, and rulers was frequently observed during the first millennium of Christianity. Even if established at the end of the Viking Age in a Scandinavia that was not yet Christian, none of these towns are surrounded by significant Old Norse grave fields.

Ships and Seafaring

The sea was a crucial channel for communication. It was always easier to travel by boat than crossing high mountains, particularly in Norway. This is why larger settlements were located on the coast. The ocean connected coastal settlements, and ships transported objects as well as people and animals. Boat-building is one of the most important identifiers of Scandinavian Vikings along with the boats and the fact that their ships were generally large. Superior ship technology enabled the projection of marine power beyond Scandinavia, and Viking vessels with armed crews were a feared arrival as they approached foreign shores.

The typical Scandinavian Viking ship was of a simple and light design. The quality of the ship building technique is particularly well demonstrated in the extraordinarily preserved ships from the ninth- and early tenth-century graves at Oseberg, Tune, and Gokstad in Norway, and the late Viking and medieval period from Roskilde fjord in Denmark. These

Figure 8. The Oseberg ship, built ca. 820.

and other finds show that Scandinavian ship technology was based on a clinker-built (*lapstrake*) technique, applying iron rivets to join long planks produced by a radial splitting of logs. The bottom planks were fastened to the keel, each plank of the hull overlapping the next, fastened with rivets to each other and to the stem-posts. The Scandinavian design, the form of the boat and rivets, and the way of joining the planks were different from that found to the south of Denmark.[54] The construction is well suited to rough sea, with integral snake-like flexibility in the hull.

Viking ships could be richly decorated. Carved wooden stem posts as on the Oseberg ship in Norway (Figure 8), or iron spirals as added to the Ladeby ship in Denmark may be mentioned. Various carvings indicate that ships could bear the head of a beast at the prow and a tail abaft. These adornments may have been removed when the ship was pulled ashore.[55]

Regarding ship technology, there was a change from the rowing of ships to combined rowing and sail around the start of the Viking Age. There is no evidence in Scandinavia that sail was employed before 800, and the Oseberg ship, dated ca. 820, is so far the earliest proof in Scandinavia for the construction of ships using sail.[56] There are strong indications that the two ships found in Salme, Estonia were built in Scandinavia, carrying men from eastern Sweden. The mid-eighth-century Salme II ship was keeled and constructed for sailing, indicating that such knowledge was already known in Sweden.[57] If wood is preserved, the origin and the date of a ship can be inferred from tree-ring analysis. Based on this method, it is suggested that the Oseberg ship was built in western Norway in 820, while Viking ships excavated in Dublin and constructed in a Scandinavian style were seemingly built locally.[58]

The main types of boat, in order of increasing size and fame, were the *faering*, the *knarr*, and the longship. The *faering* was a small open boat, ideal for fishing, featuring two pairs of oars and sometimes a rear-mounted side rudder. The *knarr* was much larger (typically around 16 × 5 m) with a side-mounted rudder and a large woollen sail. It functioned as a workhorse cargo ship sailing European and North Atlantic seaways. The longship, of course, was the archetypal Viking warship—long, narrow, and with shallow draught, built for speed and the ability to land on beaches or to navigate rivers. One such ship recovered from Roskilde Fjord in Denmark was 37 m in length and would have been manned by probably thirty-nine pairs of oars and seventy-eight oarsmen, many of whom would have doubled as Viking fighters. The longship was also steered by a side rudder (or stearing board, hence the word starboard).

Reconstruction of a sail, using old techniques and the wool from old breeds of sheep, has suggested that the fibre from five hundred animals was needed to produce an average sail. If clothes for the crew are included, then the quantity of wool and the amount of labour required are prodigious. For a *knarr*, this amounts to well over two hundred kilograms of wool and some ten person-years of work; for a warship with a crew of sixty-five to seventy men, more than 15,000 kg of wool and fifty to sixty person-years of labour would be required. An estimation of wool required for sails of the combined Danish–Norwegian Viking Age fleet amounts to one million square metres (or twelve by twelve football pitches) of sailcloth. This would require wool from around two million sheep. The sail for a vessel may actually have been worth more than the ship itself.[59]

Gender

Stereotypes of the Viking warrior or sailor have not been helpful to a full appreciation of "Viking culture" or, at least, to the role of women. It was not until the 1970s that scholars directed serious attention to the women of the Viking Age. Narratives as well as archaeological sources confirm that Viking Age Scandinavia featured a relatively strong role for both genders. This is testified in the later sagas, but contemporary graves from the Viking Age are good sources too, particularly if the skeleton is preserved (otherwise gender may have to be decided from grave goods). Some graves have typical sequences of male or female traits, but a few may be uncertain or characterized as "deviant."[60] A deviant burial, for instance, could involve someone of one gender, but containing grave goods typical of another. An example is a grave in Tønsberg, Norway, where the body had female dress accessories and no weapons, but the grave contained fishing equipment and a pair of smith's bellows.[61]

Although male graves generally outnumber those of females (indeed, female burials seem to be totally lacking in some areas), many female graves were richly equipped. The most prominent of ship graves, and probably of all Viking Age graves, the Oseberg ship burial, contained two women. This is an exceptional case, but also in Sweden some of the largest boat graves are female burials.[62]

Figure 9. Object interpreted as a seið staff, probably
belonging to a sorceress or at least a high-status woman,
Sørheim, Sogn og Fjordane, Norway.

Women and men may have had different roles, not only
regarding craft production and domestically, but also in religious life and war. While smithing and ship building would
be seen as male activities, textile production was conventionally a female one. Textile production was an important
part of Viking society—the example regarding woollen sails
illustrates the colossal resources needed in terms of material
and effort. To this should be added the clothing (mostly woollen, but other fibres like nettle and linen were also exploited).
Other roles were less clearly gendered. Both men and women
could act as merchants, for instance, as testified by balances
and weights among the goods in Scandinavian graves at
Staraya Ladoga in Russia and elsewhere.[63]

It is probable that men were more active as warriors, even
if females participated in war to a greater extent than previously assumed. Women were less physical but could contribute to combat by ritual aggression. Both genders could act
as *seiðkonur* and *seiðmen*, a kind of sorceress and sorcerer
(Figure 9).[64] These were significant social roles, in contrast to
Christian communities in which women were rarely allowed
to fill important positions.

Costume

Costume was possibly as important to the Viking identity as
fashion is to many people today. Female dress seems to have
been relatively standardized among the Norse population
throughout Scandinavia and there may have been a greater
expectation on women to maintain dress and customs in the
diaspora.[65]

Textiles and leather are not normally preserved at Viking sites, but textile tapestries and picture stones show a typical female costume as a long shift, split at the neck, under a dress. Metal accessories to fit this outfit are often found of which the most representative is the oval (tortoise) brooch. They were generally made of copper alloy and often decorated in the Viking Age style of "gripping beasts" (see below). These brooches were used to fasten the shoulder straps and worn one on each shoulder. Oval brooches started in the Merovingian period, but were not common all over Scandinavia. They had disappeared by the early Viking Age in parts of eastern Norway, and they fade from the mid-tenth century in other parts of Scandinavia. Interestingly, oval brooches of Scandinavian Viking Age type occur in Latvia in the period ca. 900–1200.[66] Additionally, female graves often contained many, sometimes hundreds, of beads. These are not specifically Scandinavian, however, and even if many were produced in Scandinavia, some of these may have been imported (Figure 10).

Male clothing was less standardized, although finds include distinctive annular (ring-shaped) or penannular (with the circumference interrupted) pins to hold cloaks in place (Figure 11). Men were probably better identified by their weapons; an expensive and strong sword, axe, or spear might be seen as part of their costume. Weapons could be elaborately decorated and inlaid with silver and gold. A full set of weapons would also include arrows and a shield. The shields could be an important identifier—thirty-two circular shields of 94 cm diameter were found in the Gokstad ship burial. They were fastened along the rail of the boat and displayed a strong colour code, alternately painted yellow and black. The same colours were added to the carvings decorating the tent and the tiller of the ship. These patterns enabled the ship to be identified from a distance, whether in foreign destinations or when returning home.

There is no evidence that people of either sex wore horned helmets!

Figure 10. Typical female dress accessories, to be found in Scandinavia and in the Viking diaspora, from Akershus, Norway.

Figure 11. Penannular pin, Hatteberg, Kvinnherad, Norway and possibly imported from Britain or Ireland.

Belief

When speaking with present-day adherents, comprehending another person's religious belief is often problematic for outsiders. This is no less so when it comes to accessing the religious ideas of the Vikings. An understanding must perforce be largely theoretical, but there are some sources to guide us. Eddic poems, such as *Voluspá*, *Grímnismál*, and *Skaldskaparmál* have been particularly important for reconstructing the belief system. They reveal different myths about the creation, the structure, and the end of life. For instance, life was created in *Ginnungagap*, a place between hot and cold domains. Cosmic elements and various divinities made things happen, and during these events gods created humans by gendering and naming two tree trunks lying on the shore—a man Ask and a woman Embla.

The world view consisted of a vertical and a horizontal axis. In the centre of the world is the vertical tree axis (Fig-

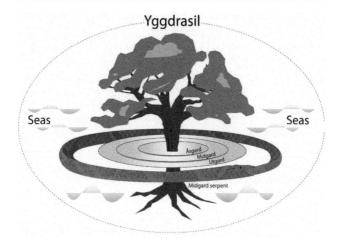

Figure 12. A cosmological model of
the Old Norse world.

ure 12). The world tree goes by several names, but *Yggdra-sil* is the best known. Along this vertical axis, communications may pass between gods, humans, and evil forces. The tree is associated with sources of wisdom and destiny. On the horizontal axis, at its centre, is *Åsgard*, the home of the gods (*Æsir*). Located outside this is *Midgard*, the domicile of humans. *Utgard* occupies the outermost zone; it is the abode of the forces of evil and chaos, including the dynasty of *jotner* (sing. *jotun*). Beyond the world are the seas and the whole is held together by one of the evil forces, the Midgard serpent. Without the serpent, the world would fall apart. The foregoing illustrates a basic principle in Old Norse religion: its dependence on forces of both good and evil. At Ragnarrǫk, the end of time, evil forces will be unleashed.[67]

The pantheon of Norse gods contains at least two tiers—the superior *æsir* and the lesser *vanir*, although *æsir* sometimes cover for both of the divine dynasties. The two groups are constantly at war, which maintains an equilibrium. The *vanir* are fertility gods and include Njordr, Freyr, and Freyja, while Þorr, Oðinn, and his son Balder are important *æsir*. Oðinn is a high god who knows magic, how to use runes and make poetry, and he receives in *Valhalla* (the "hall of the slain") all men killed during warfare. Þorr (Thor) is another important god of heaven who drives a celestial carriage accompanied by thunder and lightning. His symbol is the *Mjǫllnir* (Thor's hammer). Freyja was one of the few female goddesses and was known for her individual cultic role.

Marriages and complicated relationships took place between gods and chaos creatures like the *jotner*, and this contributed to alliances maintaining peace and fertility. An example is the marriage between Frøy, a *vanir*, and Gerd, a *jotun*. Another is Oðinn who married Frigg, with whom he produced Balder, but he also had a liaison with Jord (Earth), a *jotun*, of which Þorr was the offspring. Loki is an evil, difficult creature. He was a *jotun*, included among *æsir* when he was fostered as a brother to Oðinn.[68]

Old Norse religion was understood as a relatively uniform pan-Scandinavian phenomenon.[69] Perspectives have been changing of late and there has been an increasing emphasis on difference. Thus, we can observe variations in the distribution of names of divinities as determined through place names, and there are divergences in the nature and spread of sacred artefacts such as Thor's hammers, burials, and cult places.

Ritual Sites

How are religious ideas reflected in practice? This can be observed at burial sites. The basic characteristics of Viking Age burial customs were already in evidence in the seventh and eighth centuries, particularly in eastern Sweden. In the Viking Age they were to be enhanced, in terms of equipment and quality, all over Scandinavia. The variation demonstrated at such sites makes it difficult to conceive of some single pan-Scandinavian religion. Graves might be formed by inserting the body into a depression which was then covered by an earthen mound or a cairn of stones. Conversely, the human remains of one or more persons might be placed on the ground (or in a stone cist, wooden coffin, or boat) and covered by earth or boulders. The grave might be marked with packing stones or surrounded by a circle of stones or boulders in the shape of a ship. Burials could be inhumations, cremations, or a mixture of the two. A number of Viking Age graves include boats; the graves with larger boats often contain women rather than men. Grave goods can be absent (or have not survived), or are characterized by conspicuous wealth as at Valsgärde, Vendel in Sweden, Oseberg and Myklebust in Norway, and Ladby and Haithabu in Denmark.[70] Funerary items include weapons and dress accessories, boats, tools, religious symbols, coins, and imported artefacts. Dogs and horses are found, as well as plant remains such as apples, berries, and seeds.

Boat graves would seem to have held special significance for the Scandinavian countries, and they were dominantly inhumation graves. Although boat graves occurred outside Scandinavia, it is the concentration there which leads to the view that the spectacular sixth- and seventh-century Anglo-Saxon ship graves at Sutton Hoo in England were subject to Scandinavian influence. The tradition of putting a boat in graves seems to have started in Denmark in the second century AD. An increased frequency of boat graves began in Uppland, Sweden in the seventh century, but 80 percent of them are dated to the Viking Age. The graves during the latter period occurred particularly in Norway where many ship graves are richly furnished. The latter, with the inclusion of weapons, animals, and food, likely reflects a belief in the afterlife as recorded in written sources (e.g., Snorri Sturlusson's *Poetic Edda*).[71]

Apart from the graves, there were other types of ritual sites, as at Uppåkra and Valsgärde in Sweden, Hove and Mære in Norway, and Tissø (Figure 13) and old Lejre in Denmark.[72] Indeed, the first element of the name Tissø is the name of the war god Týr combined with the word *sø* (lake); weapons

Figure 13. A ritual site, Tissø, Denmark.

were deposited ritually in an adjacent lake. Many such places emerged before the Viking Age. Uppåkra is an example, with a stave-constructed building from the pre-Roman Iron Age, rebuilt several times, and lasting until the late Viking Age.[73] Of note are those featuring, variously, house-like structures with accumulations of activity debris, alignments of posts, cooking pits, and apparent offerings of weapons, querns, and animals. Some of these appear to represent recurrent activities lasting for up to a millennium and terminating within the Viking Age.

Much of the world to the south and west of Scandinavia at this time was Christian. Some scholars have tried to ascertain the rate at which the conversion to Christianity occurred in Scandinavia. By looking for Christian items among grave goods and studying stone crosses and cross slabs, it has been claimed that a gradual conversion occurred. Others have pointed to an abrupt break between Old Norse and Christian monuments, arguing for a top-down, forced process showing some geographical variation in conversion history. Thus, there are a few hints of gradual change in Sweden, with inhumations in former burial grounds. In Norway and Denmark, however, it seems that Christian conversion was imposed rapidly, beginning with the upper echelons of society.[74] The Christianization process started earlier in Denmark than in other parts of Scandinavia, however. Monuments at Jelling have been of particular importance for discussions about royal initiatives, and excavations during the last decade of these and of early Christian graves in Ribe have testified to the early ninth- and tenth-century presence of Christians in southern parts of Denmark. At this time, the Christians may have been primarily royal converts and foreign merchants.[75]

Art

A characteristic of the Vikings is their impressive art, with decorations on ships, weapons, dress accessories, and other objects. Dragons and other creatures were generally stylized, entwined in complicated compositions. Figures can be seen biting or grasping body parts and other decorative details, including the so-called "gripping beasts." The origin and inspiration for these is sometimes sought in Hiberno-Saxon art as exemplified by illuminated manuscripts produced in Britain or Ireland, such as the Lindisfarne Gospels (ca. 715) and the Book of Kells (ca. 800). These partly pre-date the Viking Age—indeed, the artwork has pre-Christian antecedents in its interlaced knot work and zoomorphic styles—but was produced within a Christian culture. The illustrations in these books support the accompanying gospel text. Anyone who had sight of such books, even if illiterate as the Scandinavians were at the time, would conceivably appreciate the illustrations without imbibing the Christian message.

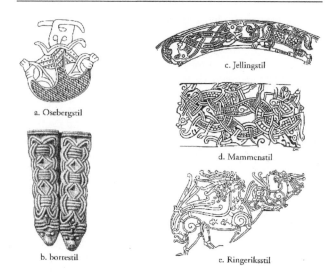

a. Osebergstil

b. borrestil

c. Jellingstil

d. Mammenstil

e. Ringeriksstil

Figure 14. A schematic overview of Viking artistic styles.

The characteristic Viking Age animal style was initially relatively simple but became more complex and formalized with time. These have been categorized, named, and dated typologically: Oseberg style (ca. 775/800–875); Borre style (ca. 850–950); Jelling style (ca. 900–975); Mammen style (ca. 960–1000/1025); Ringerike style (ca. 1050–1075); Urnes style (ca. 1050–1125).[76] In other words, the Urnes and Ringerike styles became popular after the Viking Age (Figure 14).

Similar styles are found all over Scandinavia, reflecting the diffusion of artistic ideas. Those seeing the decorations on objects from the Vendel, Valsegärde, or Oseberg graves would doubtless have been impressed by the quality of the design and artisanship. The burial at Oseberg took place in the late summer or autumn of 834, but the ship was built in 820, so at least some of the objects accompanying the women were likely of greater age than the burial. The decoration is considered to have been produced over a period and by several artists, some better than others. The character of the art indicates that the same artists could have worked on different materials, whether that be wood, bone, or metal.

State Formation in Scandinavia

Strong dynasties had begun to emerge in the Scandinavia of the sixth to seventh centuries. In the ensuing Viking Age, some petty and aspirant kings, named in written sources (such as the Kings' sagas), were competing with each other for power and resources. The modern states of Norway and Sweden did not consolidate as monarchical entities during the Viking Age, but persisted as territories with minor kingdoms for a considerable time. External threats from outside Scandinavia, in particular from a strong Germany to the south, were influential in the strengthening of Denmark's defences in the ninth century. This was perhaps one of the reasons why Denmark experienced the earliest state formation in Scandinavia.[77] Other factors may also have contributed, such as natural topography and climate. It is easier to achieve political control in a landscape like that of Denmark, compared to the rough and rocky landscape of Norway, punctuated by fjords and isolated by deep winter snows.

The state formation process in Sweden is complicated. Sigtuna was founded by King Olof Skötkonung (ca. 995–1022) or his father, Erik Segersäll, as a royal residence, hosting the first mint in Sweden and King Olof as the first Christian king. However, uprisings against Christianity and royal power were still taking place as late as the twelfth century.[78]

Harald Hårfagre (Farehair) (ca. 850–932) is conventionally presented as the founder of Norway. But his realm consisted only of parts of that country (mainly western Norway, Trøndelag, and the north), while southeastern Norway was under Danish rule. Kaupang, Norway's earliest known town, is considered to have been established by the Danes at the northern boundary of their influence, with a similar role for Hedeby in the south. Indeed, Danish control of eastern Norway may have triggered Harald Hårfagre to fight for a more extensive counterweight kingdom in Norway.[79] A rune stone at Jelling testifies to some Danish overlordship in Norway. King Harald Blåtand erected a stone monument with the following inscription:

> King Haraldr ordered these memorials to be made after Gormr, his father, and after Þórví, his mother. That Haraldr who won for himself all Denmark and Norway and made the Danes Christian.[80]

Danish kings were the strongest monarchs in Scandinavia in this period, particularly by the second half of the tenth century. Fortifications like the *Danevirke* and King Harald Blåtand's ring fortresses, reflect the ability to organize strategic defensive systems. His son, King Svend, conquered England in 1013, a project completed by Svend's son, Cnut the Great. More importantly for Scandinavia, King Cnut's realm comprised Norway too, at least in parts and for a short period (1028–35) towards the end of the Viking Age. This is significant—the Vikings raided not only outside Scandinavia, but also within it, conquering neighbours as they expanded their territorial jurisdictions.

* * *

In this chapter we have outlined some of the characteristics of Viking Age society within Scandinavia. The following chapter will go on to look at these and related traits beyond the Viking homelands.

Notes

[27] Else Roesdahl, "Aristocratic Burial in Late Viking Age Denmark. Custom, Regionality, Conversion," in *Herrschaft—Tod—Bestattung. Zu den vor- und frühgeschichtlichen Prunkgräbern als archäologisch-historische Quelle*, ed. Claus von Carnap-Borheim, Dirk Krausse, and Anke Wesse, Universitätsforsschungen Zur Prähistorischen Archäologie (Bonn: Institut für Ur- und Frühgeschichte der Universität Kiel / Habelt, 2006), 169–83; Sæbjørg Walaker Nordeide, "Where Did All the People Go? Looking for Eleventh-Century Graves in Southern Norway," in *Viking Settlements and Viking Society. Papers from the Proceedings of the 16th Viking Congress,*

Reykjavík and Reykholt, 16–23 August 2009, ed. Svavar Sigmunds-son (Reykjavík: Hid Islenzka Fornleifafélag / University of Iceland Press, 2011), 320–32.

[28] Karin Fjellhammer Seim, "Runologi," in *Handbok i norrøn filologi*, ed. Odd Einr Haugen (Bergen: Fabokforlaget, 2004), 119–74.

[29] Else Roesdahl, "Walrus Ivory—Demand, Supply, Workshops, and Greenland," in *Viking and Norse in the North Atlantic: Select Papers from the Proceedings of the Fourteenth Viking Congress Tórshavn, 19–30 July 2001*, ed. Andras Mortensen and Símun V. Arge (Tórshavn: Føroya, 2005), 182–91.

[30] Bente Magnus, "Fisker eller bonde? Undersøkelser av hus-tufter på ytterkysten," *Viking* for 1974 (1974): 68–108.

[31] Inga-Maria Mulk and Inger Zachrisson, "Samerna under tidig järnålder–tidig medeltid," in *Arkeologi i Norden*, ed. Göran Buren-hult, 2 vols. (Stockholm: Natur & Kultur, 1999–2000), 2:378–79; Hansen and Olsen, *Samenes historie*, 102–3.

[32] Jan Klápste and Anne Nissen Jaubert, "Rural Settlement," in *The Archaeology of Medieval Europe, 1: Eighth to Twelfth Centuries AD*, ed. James Graham-Campbell, Acta Jutlandica Humanities Series 83.1 (Aarhus: Aarhus University Press, 2007), 76–110; Jan-Henrik Fallgren, "Farm and Village in the Viking Age," in *The Viking World*, ed. Stefan Brink (London: Routledge, 2008), 67–76.

[33] Lars Jørgensen, "Kongsgård—kultsted—marked. Overve-jelser omkring Tissøkompleksets struktur og Funktion," in *Plats och praxis: Studier av nordisk förkristen ritual*, ed. Kristina Jennbert, Anders Andrén, and Catharina Raudvere, Vägar till Midgård (Lund: Nordic, 2002), 215–47; Joachim Schultze, "Aspects of Settlement Structure and House Construction in Hedeby," in *Viking Settle-ments and Viking Society. Papers from the Proceedings of the 16th Viking Congress, Reykjavík and Reykholt, 16–23 August 2009*, ed. Svavar Sigmundsson (Reykjavík: Hid Islenzka Fornleifafélag / Uni-versity of Iceland Press, 2011), 375–92.

[34] Fallgren, "Farm and Village in the Viking Age"; Anne Ped-ersen, "Vikingetidsfund fra Limfjordsområdet," in *Aggersborg i Vikingetiden: Bebyggelsen og Borgen*, ed. Else Roesdahl, Søren M. Sindbæk, and Anne Pedersen (Højbjerg: Jysk Arkæologisk Selskab, 2014), 31–46.

[35] Kurt *Schietzel, Spurensuche Haithabu: archäologische Spuren-suche in der frühmittelalterlichen Ansiedlung Haithabu. Dokumenta-tion und Chronik, 1963–2013* (Neumünster: Wachholtz, 2014), 120.

[36] Anne Nørgård Jørgensen, Lars Jørgensen, and Lone Gebauer Thomsen, "Assembly Sites for Cult, Markets, Jurisdiction and Social

Relations. Historic-Ethnological Analogy between North Scandinavian Church Towns, Old Norse Assembly Sites and Pit House Sites of the Late Iron Age and Viking Period," *Arkæologi i Slesvig / Archäologie in Schleswig: Sonderband "Det 61. Internationale Sachsensymposion 2010" Haderslev, Danmark*, ed. Linda Boye et al. (Neumünster: Wachholtz, 2011), 95–112.

[37] Gerd Stamsø Munch, Olav Sverre Johansen, and Else Roesdahl, eds., *Borg in Lofoten: A Chieftain's Farm in North Norway*, Arkeologisk Skriftserie 1 (Trondheim: Tapir, 2003).

[38] Else Roesdahl, Søren M. Sindbæk, and Anne Pedersen, eds., *Aggersborg i Vikingetiden: Bebyggelsen og Borgen*, Jysk Arkæologisk Selskabs Skrifter (Højbjerg: Jysk Arkæologisk Selskab, 2014), 442–63; T. Douglas Price et al., "Who Was in Harold Bluetooth's Army? Strontium Isotope Investigation of the Cemetery at the Viking Age Fortress at Trelleborg, Denmark," *Antiquity* 85 (2011): 476–89.

[39] Fallgren, "Farm and Village in the Viking Age."

[40] Stefan Brink, "Skiringssal, Kaupang, Tjølling—the Toponymic Evidence," in *Kaupang in Skiringssal*, ed. Dagfinn Skre (Århus: Aarhus University Press, 2007), 53–64; Stefan Brink in collaboration with Neil Price, eds., *The Viking World* (London: Routledge, 2008).

[41] The Viking World, ed. Brink, 57–66.

[42] Lisbeth Eilersgaard Christensen, Thorsten Lemm, and Anne Pedersen, eds., *Husebyer—Status Quo, Open Questions and Perspectives. Papers from a Workshop at the National Museum, Copenhagen 19–20 March 2014*, Publications from the National Museum. Studies in Archaeology & History. Jelling Series 20.3 (Copenhagen: National Museum, 2016).

[43] Magnus Olsen, *Ættegård og Helligdom* (1926; Bergen: Universitetsforlaget, 1978).

[44] Stefan Brink, "How Uniform Was the Old Norse Religion?," in *Learning and Understanding in the Old Norse World*, ed. Judy Quinn, Kate Heslop, and Tarrin Wills, Medieval Texts and Cultures of Northern Europe (Turnhout: Brepols, 2007), 105–36.

[45] Silke Eisenschmidt, "The Viking Age Graves from Hedeby," in *Viking Settlements and Viking Society. Papers from the Proceedings of the 16th Viking Congress, Reykjavík and Reykholt, 16–23 August 2009*, ed. Svavar Sigmundsson (Reykjavík: Hid Islenzka Fornleifafélag / University of Iceland Press, 2011), 83–102; Schietzel, *Spurensuche Haithabu*, 165; Silke Eisenschmidt, *Grabfunde des 8. Bis 11. Jahrhunderts zwischen Kongeå und Eider: Zur Bestattungssitte der Wikingerzeit im südlichen Altdänemark*, Studien zur

Siedlungsgeschichte und Archäologie der Ostseegebiete 5, 2 vols. (Neumünster: Wachholz 2004).

46 Claus Feveile, "Ribe på nordsiden av åen, 8.–12. Århundrede," in *Ribe Studier: Det ældste Ribe. Udgravninger på nordsiden af Ribe Å 1984-2000*, ed. Claus Feveile, Jysk Arkæologisk Selskabs Skrifter (Højbjerg: Jysk arkæologisk selskab, 2006), 134-63; Morten Søvsø, "Ribes ældste gravpladser, ca. 700–1050," in *Død og begravet—i Vikingetiden: Artikler fra et seminar på Københavns Universitet den 26. februar 2016*, ed. Jens Ulriksen and Henriette Lyngstrøm (Copenhagen: SAXO-instituttet, Københavns Universitet, 2016), 149-59, available online at www.vikingfregerslev.dk/Files/Billeder/FREGERSLEV_KAMMERGRAV/Artikler/Ryttergraven-i-Fregerslev-et-uopklaret-mysterium.pdf.

47 Olaf Olsen, "Introduktion," in *Kristendommen i Danmark før 1050*, ed. Niels Lund (Roskilde: Roskilde Museum, 2004), 1-4; Søvsø, "Ribes ældste gravpladser, ca. 700–1050."

48 Björn Ambrosiani, "Birka," in *The Viking World*, ed. Brink, 94-100; Jonas Ros, *Sigtuna: Staden, kyrkorna och den kyrkliga organisationen*, Opia (Occasional Papers in Archaeology) 30 (Uppsala: Uppsala University, 2001).

49 Dagfinn Skre, "The Development of Urbanism in Scandinavia," in *The Viking World*, ed. Brink, 83-93.

50 Brita Malmer, "South Scandinavian Coinage in the Ninth Century," in *Silver Economy in the Viking Age*, ed. James Graham-Campbell and Gareth Williams (New York: Routledge, 2007), 13-27.

51 Henrik Klackenberg, *Moneta nostra: Monetarisering i medeltidens Sverige*, Lund Studies in Medieval Archaeology 10 (Lund: Almqvist & Wiksell International, 1992), 20-25; Brita Malmer, "Kristna symboler på Danska mynt ca. 825-1050," in *Kristendommen i Danmark før 1050*, ed. Lund, 75-85; Brita Malmer, J. Ros, and S. Tesch, *Kung Olofs mynthus i kvarteret Urmakaren, Sigtuna*, Sigtuna Museers Skriftserie 3 (Sigtuna: Sigtuna museum, 1991), 13-14; Svein Gullbekk, "Review: Brita Malmer, The Anglo-Scandinavian Coinage c. 995-1020 [...]," *British Numismatic Journal* 67 (1997): 154-55.

52 Else Roesdahl, ed. *Viking og Hvidekrist: Norden og Europa 800-1200* (Copenhagen: Nordisk Ministerråd, Europarådet, 1992), 310; Simún Arge, "Í Uppistovubeitinum. Site and Settlement," *Froðskaparrit* 45 (1997): 27-44.

53 Peter Carelli, "Lunds åldsta kyrkogård och förekomsten av ett senvikingatida danskt parochialsystem," in *Kristendommen i Danmark før 1050*, ed. Lund, 253-58; Sæbjørg Walaker Nordeide and

Steinar Gulliksen, "First Generation Christians, Second Generation Radiocarbon Dates: The Cemetery at St. Clement's in Oslo," *Norwegian Archaeological Review* 40, no. 1 (2007): 1–25; Søvsø, "Ribes ældste gravpladser, ca. 700–1050."

[54] Ole Crumlin-Pedersen, "Ship Types and Sizes AD 800–1400," in *Aspects of Maritime Scandinavia, AD 200—1200*, ed. Ole Crumlin-Pedersen (Roskilde: The Viking Ship Museum, 1991), 69–82.

[55] Anne Christine Sørensen, *Ladby: A Danish Ship-Grave from the Viking Age*, Ships and Boats of the North 3 (Roskilde: The Viking Ship Museum, 2001), 46–47.

[56] Niels Bonde, "De Norske Vikingeskipbsgraves Alder. Et vellykket norsk-dansk forskningsprosjekt," *Nationalmuseets Arbejdsmark* for 1994 (1994): 128–47.

[57] T. Douglas Price, Jüri Peets, Raili Allmäe, Liina Maldre, and Ester Oras, "Isotopic Provenancing of the Salme Ship Burials in Pre-Viking Age Estonia," *Antiquity* 90 (2016): 1022–37.

[58] Niels Bonde and Frans-Arne Stylegar, "Fra Avaldsnes til Oseberg. Dendrokronologiske undersøkelser av skipsgravene fra Storhaug og Grønhaug på Karmøy," *Viking* for 2009 (2009): 149–68; Ruth Johnson, *Viking Age Dublin* (Dublin: TownHouse, 2014), 75.

[59] Lise Bender Jørgensen, "The Introduction of Sails to Scandinavia: Raw Materials, Labour and Land," in *N-Tag Ten. Proceedings of the 10th Nordic Tag Conference at Stiklestad, Norway 2009*, ed. Ragnhild Berge, Marek E. Jasinski, and Kalle Sognnes, British Archaeological Reports International Series 2399 (Oxford: Archaeopress, 2012), 173–81 at 173.

[60] E. M. Murphy, *Deviant Burial in the Archaeological Record* (Oxford: Oxbow, 2008).

[61] Sæbjørg Walaker Nordeide, *The Viking Age as a Period of Religious Transformation: The Christianization of Norway from AD 560–1150/1200*, Studies in Viking and Medieval Scandinavia 2 (Turnhout: Brepols, 2011), 262–65.

[62] Bergljot Solberg, *Jernalderen i Norge. Ca. 500 f.Kr.–1030 e.Kr.* (Oslo: Cappelen, 2003), 223; Gunilla Larsson, *Ship and Society: Maritime Ideology in Late Iron Age Sweden*, Aun: Archaeological Studies / Uppsala University Institute of North European Archaeology 37 (Uppsala: Department of Archaeology and Ancient History, Uppsala University, 2007), 371.

[63] Anne Stalsberg, "Tradeswomen during the Viking Age," in *Nordic TAG: Report from the 2nd Nordic TAG Conference, Umeå, 1987*, ed. Evert Baoudou (Umeå: Department of Archaeology, University of Umeå, 1992), 45–52.

[64] Neil S. Price, *The Viking Way: Religion and War in Late Iron Age Scandinavia*, Aun 31 (Uppsala: Department of Archaeology and Ancient History, University of Uppsala, 2002), 389–91; Leszek Gardela, "'Warrior-Women' in Viking Age Scandinavia? A Preliminary Archaeological Study," in *Funeral Archaeology*, ed. Slawomir Kardow, Analecta Archaeologica. Ressoviensia (Rzeszów: Intitute og Archaeology, Reszów University, 2013), 273–314.

[65] Clare Downham, "Viking Ethnicities: A Historiographic Overview," *History Compass* 10, no. 1 (2012): 1–12.

[66] Roberts Spirgis, "Liv Tortois Brooches in the Lower Daugava Area in the 10th–13th Centuries," in *Cultural Interaction between East and West: Archaeology, Artefacts and Human Contacts in Northern Europe*, ed. Ulf Fransson et al., Stockholm Studies in Archaeology (Stockholm: Stockholm University, 2007), 197—204; Nordeide, *The Viking Age as a Period of Religious Transformation*, 262–65.

[67] Gro Steinsland, *Norrøn religion: myter, riter, samfunn* (Oslo: Pax, 2005), 96–106.

[68] Steinsland, *Norrøn religion*, passim.

[69] Anders Andrén, *Tracing Old Norse Cosmology: The World Tree, Middle Earth, and the Sun from Archaeological Perpectives*, Vägar till Midgård 16 (Lund: Nordic, 2014).

[70] Jensen, *Danmarks Oldtid*, 336; Sørensen, *Ladby*; Eisenschmidt, *Grabfunde des 8. Bis 11. Jahrhunderts zwischen Kongeå und Eider*; A. W. Brøgger, Hjalmar Falk, and Haakon Shetelig, eds., *Osebergfundet*, 4 vols. (Oslo: Den Norske Stat / Universitetets Oldsaksamling, 1917–), esp. vol. 1; John Ljungkvist, "Valsgärde—Development and Change of a Burial Ground over 1300 Years," in *Valsgärde Studies: The Place and Its People, Past and Present*, ed. Svante Norr, Occasional Papers in Archaeology (Uppsala: Department of Archaeology and Ancient History, Uppsala University, 2008), 13–55.

[71] Jenny-Rita Næss, "Grav i båt eller båt i grav," *Stavanger Museums Årbok* (1969): 57–76; Solberg, *Jernalderen i Norge*, 223.

[72] Oddmunn Farbregd, "Hove i Åsen. Kultstad og bygdesentrum," *Spor*, no. 2 (1986): 42–46, 50–51; Jørgensen, "Kongsgård—kultsted—marked"; Lars Larsson, "The Iron Age Ritual Building at Uppåkra, Southern Sweden," *Antiquity* 81 (March 2007): 11–25; John Ljungkvist, "Valsgärde."

[73] Larsson, "The Iron Age Ritual Building at Uppåkra."

[74] Tore Artelius and Anna Kristensson, "The Universe Container. Projections of Religious Meaning in a Viking Age Burial-Ground in

Northern Småland," in *Old Norse Religion in Long-Term Perspectives: Origins, Changes, and Interactions*, ed. Anders Andrén, Kristina Jennbert, and Catharina Raudvere, Vägar till Midgård (Lund: Nordic, 2006), 147–52; Roesdahl, "Aristocratic Burial in Late Viking Age Denmark"; Nordeide, *The Viking Age as a Period of Religious Transformation*, 321.

75 Knud J. Krogh, *Gåden om Kong Gorms Grav: Historien om Nordhøjen i Jelling*, Vikingekongernes Monumenter i Jelling 1 (Herning: Carlsbergfondet og Nationalmuseet 1993); Mads Dengsø Jessen et al., "A Palisade Fit for a King: Ideal Architecture in King Harald Bluetooth's Jelling," *Norwegian Archaeological Review* 47, no. 1 (2014): 42–64; Morten Søvsø, "Tidligkristne Begravelser ved Ribe Domkirke—Ansgars Kirkegård?," in *Symposium Jarplund*, ed. Sunhild Kleingärtner, Signe Lützau Pedersen, and Lilian Matthes, Arkæologi i Slesvig (Neumünster: Wachholtz, 2010), 147–64; Søvsø, "Ribes ældste gravpladser, ca. 700–1050"; Olaf Olsen, "Introduktion," in *Kristendommen i Danmark før 1050*, ed. Lund, 1–4.

76 James Graham-Campbell, *Viking Art, World of Art* (London: Thames & Hudson, 2013), 9.

77 Sverre Bagge, *From Viking Stronghold to Christian Kingdom: State Formation in Norway, c. 900–1350* (Copenhagen: Museum Tusculanum Press, 2010).

78 Nils Blomkvist, Stefan Brink, and Thomas Lindkvist, "The Kingdom of Sweden," in *Christianization and the Rise of Christian Monarchy*, ed. Nora Berend (Cambridge: Cambridge University Press, 2007), 167–213.

79 Dagfinn Skre, ed., *Kaupang in Skiringssal*, Kaupang Excavation Project Publication Series 1 (Århus: Aarhus University Press, 2007), 445–69; Bagge, *From Viking Stronghold to Christian Kingdom*, 23–25.

80 Michael P. Barnes, "The Scandinavian Languages in the Viking Age," in *The Viking World*, ed. Brink, 274–80 at 277.

Chapter 3

The Viking Diaspora

In searching for the Vikings beyond their Scandinavian homelands, it would probably be unwise to rely on the ability of indigenous, non-Norse peoples to distinguish between Swedes, Danes, and Norwegians. Post-Viking sources may tell us about "dark/black" and "fair/white dressed foreigners," referring to Danes and Norwegians respectively, but this is not definitive as to place of origin.[81] Arguably, such distinctions are not very important when looking for "the Vikings" in general. It is more problematic if non-Scandinavians are recorded as Vikings or Scandinavians. Human DNA research has been a key research tool for characterizing biological ancestry, although genetic composition says nothing about a person's culture and social codes. It does provide clues as to whether men and women migrated, or whether it was mainly the adult men who then associated with the women of the territories to which they travelled.

Physical surroundings can, however, influence the body—even if a person moves, the location in which they grew up may still be traceable from isotope analyses of their skeletal remains. Knowledge of environmental and climatic change, studied through the approaches of such fields as geomorphology (landform history), pedology (soil science), and palynology (pollen analysis) produce information regarding when and how people affected their environment or were influenced by it. Scientific data on soils, vegetation, and crops, for instance, can furnish evidence of what Scan-

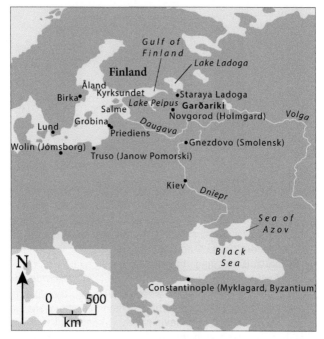

Figure 15. Map of eastern Europe with waterways to Constantinople.

dinavians were doing in the diaspora, as well as at home in Scandinavia. Were they just raiding or trading, or did they become settled farmers? In the pristine landscapes of the North Atlantic, to what extent can a colonizing imprint be determined? We will consider these and other topics below.

The Eastward Expansion

Even if Finland is the closest neighbour to Scandinavia (Figure 15), its history and languages are different. There are no written sources from Viking Age Finland, and the chronology of the languages is complex. During historical times, there have been Swedish, Finnish, Sámi, and Russian-speaking people who all, except those speaking Swedish, would have had problems when communicating with Scandinavians. Swedes started to settle in mainland Finland from before the beginning of the Viking Age. Only small areas of modern Finland were permanently settled, and most of the country was a wilderness used for hunting, fishing, and trapping. There are no obvious signs of Scandinavian colonies, and there is no evidence that the Finns took part in the Viking voyages, except from Åland. This archipelago, today part of Finland, is considered a contact zone between Finland and Scandinavia, and the graves and material culture of Viking Age Åland are totally Scandinavian in character.[82]

Circular brooches were normal dress accessories in western Finland. Tortoise brooches, standard in Scandinavia in the Viking Age, became fashionable only at the end of the Viking Age in eastern Finland where they were decorated with plant motifs rather than with Scandinavian-style animals. The two-edged sword, long-handled axe, and the spear were the most important weapons, as in Scandinavia, but while silver became very popular in the latter, it was rare in Finland other than on Åland. This suggests that medieval Åland should be considered part of Scandinavia; the rest of Finland was only loosely associated with Viking activity. This was so in spite of the fact that the south coast of Finland was on the Viking route eastwards, and a craft and trading centre emerged near Kyrksundet in the Hiittinen archipelago. This centre is, however, mostly dated to the second half of the (post-Viking Age) eleventh century.[83]

Scandinavians took advantage of waterways as far as they could, transporting people and commodities at the same time as travelling. They crossed the Baltic Sea and entered rivers and inlets on the Baltic coast. From Sweden people journeyed, via the island of Gotland in all probability, to the Eastern Baltic (modern-day Estonia, Latvia, and Lithuania). A major route was along Latvia's Daugava River, another was through the Gulf of Finland, following the coast of Estonia into Lake Peipus via the River Nara, or further along the Gulf to Lake Ladoga in Russia. Lake Ladoga was a contact zone

Figure 16. Part of grave field with barrows
by the river in Staraya Ladoga.

between diverse cultures at this time.[84] From here, Scandinavians could move inland along rivers such as the Volkhov.
Rowing, sailing, or portage would enable access to the Volga
and Dniepr rivers and thence to places like Staraya Ladoga
and Novgorod in Russia, and beyond to Kiev and Constantinople (present-day Istanbul), with travellers given names like
Rus and Varangian *en route* (see Chapter 1).

While there is abundant evidence of Viking activity to
the east, the fact that the number of Scandinavian artefacts
found in eastern Europe is very high compared to western
Europe including the British Isles, is not generally known.
They outnumber the quantity of Viking Age artefacts found
in Denmark for instance, and they represent a range of activities ascribable to both men and women.[85] Former political
conflicts between countries to the west and the east during
the twentieth-century Cold War, with a relative lack of access
to the east, may account for the lacunae in knowledge, but
the situation is now much improved. This is fortunate because
sources for Viking Age history in eastern Europe are considerable. Not only is the archaeology there rich, but Arabic written sources regarding Scandinavian migration to the east are

copious yet have received little attention.[86] Language skills may have proved a barrier for researchers, but a lack of personal names and identifiable individuals may have contributed to the dearth of interest for these sources among historians.

It would seem that Scandinavians *en masse* travelled earlier towards the east than venturing further south or west. One theory, advanced by Duczko in 2004, is that it was merchants from central Sweden who travelled eastwards in order to buy high-quality furs. According to this theory, the Scandinavian activity increased considerably from the middle of the eighth century, creating the need for a common meeting place—hence the foundation of Staraya Ladoga on the River Volkhov (Figure 16). From about 850 the number of Scandinavian immigrants, including more warriors, increased. The military involvement is exemplified by an unsuccessful attack on Constantinople of a Scandinavian army in June 860.[87] There is also evidence for the significant presence of a Norse female population in the east, and women may have acted as merchants.

The earliest layers of settlement from important sites like Staraya Ladoga are from the mid-eighth century, and graves with Scandinavian artefacts are found from the seventh to ninth centuries at Grobina, Priediens, Porāni, and Rudzukalns.[88] A hoard from Supruty in Upper Oka included a bridle decorated in Borre style, but with parallels in central Sweden and Gotland.[89] In Kiev a hoard has recently been found containing six gold bracelets with Scandinavian affinities, and Islamic coins date the hoard to post-905/6.[90] We can find frequent occurrences of Thor's hammer rings, testifying that cult and beliefs associated with Norse religion followed the Scandinavians. Such hammer rings are typical of central Sweden where more than four hundred have been found. A Scandinavian presence is witnessed further by a runic inscription on a stone on the island of Berezan at the mouth of the Dnieper. This is the only rune stone known from eastern Europe, and records that "Grane made this sarcophagus for Karl, his partner."[91]

The finds from Salme in Estonia (see Chapters 1 and 2) are dated to around 750. Forty-one men were killed there and buried in two ship graves located at the shore-side. Grave goods included high quality weapons and other precious grave goods. Isotope (especially strontium) and artefact analyses indicate that they likely came from the Stockholm–Mälaren region of central Sweden. Given that they were buried with full ceremony, it has been posited that the area may have been under Swedish control at the time of their internment.[92] Armed men in several ships, with little more than gaming pieces for on-board entertainment and potential gifts, could be a prototype for how a Viking raid was equipped. Whoever dealt the fatal blows at Salme, this indicates that the Swedes started raiding and colonizing eastwards no later than the middle of the eighth century, and probably earlier.

Vikings were a key ingredient in so-called *emporia*, the early, eastern towns. Apart from being settlers, they also visited as merchants and craft-workers, probably travelling between Scandinavian emporia such as Birka, Ribe, Hedeby, and Kaupang. Wolin in Poland was another place where a significant number of Scandinavian artefacts have been found and it may be the location of "Jómsborg," mentioned by Adam of Bremen, a German eleventh-century chronicler, and Snorri Sturlusson, the Icelandic poet, historian, and law-yer of the twelfth and thirteenth centuries. Janów Pomor-ski near the Pomeranian coast has been identified as the port of "Truso," cited in writings by Wulfstan, simultaneously (from 1002) Archbishop of York and Bishop of London and Worcester. There, remains of Scandinavian settlement have been revealed—typical longhouses and clinker-built boats, together with traces of various crafts. This all indicates a substantial Scandinavian presence along the eastern Baltic shores, including men, women and the carrying out of a variety of activities, not only raiding. Generally strong, dynastic connections existed between the Piast dynasty rulers of Poland and Scandinavian elites. The finds are indicative of a population predominantly from Gotland, eastern Sweden, and Denmark.[93]

Further afield, Arabic sources allow us to deduce that the Scandinavian Rus fostered commercial and political organization. Ahmad Ibn Faḍlān, a well-known Arabic author and traveller, produced vivid descriptions of people with a Scandinavian background and their traditions (Text Box 2). The Rus represented an important connection between western Europe and areas to the east. Geographically, Arabic informants locate the Rus to an area north of the Caucasus and south of the historical territory of Volga Bulgaria, and also bounded to the west by the town of Azov on a Crimean inlet of the Black Sea and on the east by the Caspian Sea.

The Rus as a people can be separated into two groups. The Kievan Rus were probably dominantly Slavic and the Volga–Caspian Rus were probably mainly Scandinavian. Both groups contained immigrant merchants and warriors, but they were eventually acculturated with the local Slavs. It is also argued, however, that Kiev was founded by Rus, and Byzantine records tell us that Norsemen called *Rhos* ruled over *Rhossia*. They apparently took tribute from Slavic tribes, and were led by a group of twenty people, all with Norse names. The Scandinavian identity of these people was maintained for a while, but eventually faded and it seems generally to have been weaker among the Kievan Rus than elsewhere. The impact on archaeological material is more diffuse than in written sources, and in 940 a member of the elite first bears a Slavic name.[94]

Scandinavians travelled all the way to Constantinople— as famously did Harald Hardrada (Haraldr Hardráði, King of Norway from 1046) who spent several years as a mercenary in *Garðariki* (which appears to denote a large area within present-day Russia and Ukraine) and Byzantium. This was the same Harald Hardrada who was defeated by King Harold Godwinson in 1066 at the Battle of Stamford Bridge in Yorkshire.[95] Several runic inscriptions in Hagia Sophia offer further evidence of the Norse presence in Constantinople during the Viking Age, probably recording the male names Halftan and Árni. Silk found in various Scandinavian graves, particularly at Oseberg and Birka, confirms connections between China and Scandinavia, doubtless via the Silk Road and Constantinople, and thence following riverine trade routes.

Evidence for Scandinavians is not evenly distributed across the lands between the Baltic and the Caspian Sea, but is mainly found in towns and along the routes mentioned above. Beyond this, a few Viking artefacts, but no settlements, are known from the Balkans. Most material represents stray finds and all artefacts are from a brief period (the second half of the tenth to the beginning of the eleventh century), consisting largely of weapons. These may have arrived along the Danube as a result of military raids, for instance in 968 and 969–971 by Sviatoslav, Grand Prince of Kiev and someone with a Scandinavian origin; or they may have been brought by Scandinavian mercenaries and merchants associated with the Byzantine army.[96]

The Southward Expansion

The Vikings followed the seas and other waterways around Europe and down to the Mediterranean. The impact on the European mainland was not great overall, although the situation varies; Normandy, for instance, derives its name from "northmen" (as seen in Chapter 2).

Archaeological sources are sparse, and written sources are not straightforward:

> It has often proved impossible to confirm the places and dates of Viking raids, to document the effect of these raids on local communities, or to evaluate the role played in deterring Viking raids by the physical defences and fleets that were constructed in this period. The more detailed the stories of Vikings are, the less we are inclined to believe in them.[97]

Activity around the Iberian Peninsula and in the Mediterranean seems to have been limited to raiding on a minor scale from the ninth to the eleventh centuries, and no Scandinavian settlements have been identified.[98] Only a few possible Scandinavian items have survived from the Viking Age and the Arabic coins found in Scandinavia were not minted in Moorish Iberia (al-Andalus). The first record of an attack there was in 844 after Vikings from Norway had started to over-winter on the Loire in France. So, these attacks may not have been organized from Scandinavia directly.

In the period between 799 and 843, "Northmen" repeatedly attacked areas on the west coast of France, particularly around Noirmoutier. "Nordmannia" and "Nordmanni" seem to have meant "Denmark" and "Danes." There is no mention of anyone being massacred, raped, or captured as slaves in this area; rather there are reports formulated in an ironic style, telling how the raiders were trying to "capture some monks" who were subjected to "painful acts of scorn and mockery."[99] It seems that the Vikings were not marauding for ecclesiastical treasures and precious metal, but rather for salt. This commodity was also sought by merchants from Britain and Ireland, but they seemed to have been trading rather than raiding.[100]

Normandy was established as a Scandinavian polity under their leader Rollo in the tenth century. The identity of Rollo has been debated,[101] questioning whether he was of Danish descent or to be identified with the Norwegian chieftain *"Gange-Rolf."*[102] The Carolingians had engaged Rollo as part of a strategy to repel subsequent Viking incursions and especially to defend "maritime parts" at Rouen, which probably meant the port area. A number of Viking camps are known near several of the larger rivers in France, and a few place names witness transitory Scandinavian settlements which do not appear to have survived beyond the first half of the tenth century.

If the colonization of Normandy was short-lived and not extensive, it was even less successful in Brittany. The only Viking grave known in France was found there in 1906 on the island Ile de Groix. This was a cremation grave for two individuals, dated to the first half of the tenth century. Grave goods included weapons and tools with an origin in Norway and a suggestion of time spent in other parts of western Europe.

Frisia which at that time covered much of what is today the coastal part of the Netherlands did, however, attract Scandinavian warlords: Harald Klak was granted Rüstringen in 826,

Walcheren in 841, and his brother Rorik conquered Dorestadt in 850 and was granted rulership in southern Frisia.

The Viking impact on the western parts of the European mainland may have contributed positively to the economies of previously raided polities as well as to Scandinavia, but it was clearly unwelcome to those who had been attacked.[103] The cultural and political shock to these regions was on a lesser scale than was to be found in certain areas to the west.

The Westward Expansion

Many different groups migrated to the island of Great Britain subsequent to its final separation from the European mainland ca. 6000 BC (Ireland was likely a separate island prior to the Late Glacial era). Since prehistoric times—and perhaps during them—incomers to Britain and Ireland, as elsewhere, might be viewed, variously, as invaders, colonisers, settlers, immigrants, or refugees. Such terms are contested and depend on motivations and perspectives. There is little doubt that Angles, Saxons, Jutes, Danes, and Norwegians were seen as unwelcome to many members of indigenous groups, just as much as the Romans were prior to this and the Normans afterwards. In terms of Scandinavians, there is unquestionable evidence for their raiding and colonization. Scandinavians are traced in urban and rural settlements, graves, and artefacts. In addition, written sources such as place names, laws, documents, and runes testify to their presence.

Substantial colonization took place in the Scottish islands, eastern England, and southern Ireland. While Norwegians dominated activities in Scotland and Ireland, the Danes were the primary Scandinavian settlers in England.[104] Yet no Viking longship has been found in Britain. They must have been used to transport Vikings, probably with *knarrs* for cargo-based support, between the British Isles and Scandinavia. But the survival of a predominantly wooden vessel would be problematic unless boats were preserved in graves. A different possibility is that many Norse people probably returned to their homeland with such ships. For the very late Viking period, a longship retrieved from Roskilde in Denmark (Skuldelev 2) was revealed by tree-ring analysis to have been probably built in the Dublin area of eastern Ireland around 1042. Dendrochronology dates a different ship, Skuldelev 6, to around 1025, with construction in the Oslofjord area of Norway, repairs in the vicinity of the Baltic Sea, before its eventual demise in Denmark.[105] We can see here how truly international the Viking Age marine community was.

Place names may tell us more about Viking settlement than any other evidence. Viking burials, houses, and arte-facts are far less numerous in Britain than Norse place names. Norse names, for instance, represent the vast major-ity of forms in Shetland, Orkney, and Caithness. Names end-ing in -staðir, -setr, -bolstaðr, -kví, -hamarr, -bú, -ey, -holm, and -ford are frequent and may be typical of Norwegian origins, and they are also found in western Scotland, Cumbria, and the Isle of Man. Danish elements are more common in the Danelaw of eastern England, as instanced in such suffixes as -by, -thorpe, -toft, and -thwaite. Some names are found in both areas (cf. -wick, -kirk, -nes, -dalr).

Ireland

According to the *Annals of Ulster* (Irish: *Annála Uladh*) the first Viking attack on Ireland took place in 795, and sporadic raids continued until 837 when sixty ships appeared on the riv-ers Liffey and Boyne, with the plundering of churches, forts, and dwellings. In 839, Scandinavians over-wintered for the first time (beside Lough Neagh in the north of the island). Fortified river-side or coastal settlements—*longphorts* ("ship-camps")—formed important bases for Scandinavian activity, some of which became permanent (e.g., Dublin, Waterford, Wexford, Cork, and Limerick). All these sites had good har-bours and easy access to the sea. From 841 it was clear that the incomers would stay, founding permanent centres in Dub-lin and Linn Duachaill, near Annagassan in Co. Louth. Indeed, most of the important Scandinavian settlements in Ireland

Figure 17. Reconstruction of an urban house from Dublin, Ireland.

in the ninth century were of urban character or became so. Very few Norse sites are known outside present-day towns, and only one possible boat-burial. It has been suggested that Dublin may have been the capital of a sea-kingdom, encompassing the Isle of Man, much of the western seaboard of Scotland, and Cumbria.[106]

The nature of the relationship between the Vikings and the formation of towns is uncertain—they both appeared on the Irish scene at the same time, but it is unclear if the Vikings caused the urbanization, or if this process was already underway.

Excavations in Dublin are particularly rich in information regarding Scandinavian settlement. The old Viking Age and medieval town was located by the mouth of the River Liffey with its natural harbour. Houses and decorated objects encourage speculation as to the degree of co-existence between Norse and indigenous people (Figure 17). Wooden objects carved with Hiberno-Saxon as well as Scandinavian ornamentation, and sometimes both, are found in the same contexts. This suggests that native Irish and Norse peoples lived in close proximity, working together, or learning from each other. The Norse, like the Irish (whose Iron Age and early medieval periods were aceramic), did not produce pottery, but used stave-constructed wooden bowls instead, keeping up the tradition from their homeland, which in the Irish Scandinavians' case would most likely be Norway. At least forty graves with assumed Norse bodies from the ninth century are found around the town. The majority were inhumations, but they had grave goods of mainly Scandinavian and non-Christian type. Most graves contained weapons and few featured the typical oval brooches identifying a Scandinavian Viking Age woman. From this it could be deduced that far more Norse men than women moved to Ireland. It should be borne in mind, however, that a similar gender pattern is demonstrated in Scandinavia where the issue of colonial demography would not apply. Leaving aside any questions of unequal survival of evidence for female burials, it might be noted that female infanticide was allowable in pre-Christian Scandinavia and this could be part of the explanation of uneven gender representation among Hiberno-Scandinavian graves in both Scandinavia and the Viking diaspora.

DNA evidence from modern Irish populations suggests a maximum of around 20 percent Norwegian ancestry within Ireland, but no lower limit was determinable. Viking immigrants to Ireland are inferred to have originated predominantly from the north and west coast of Norway. Ireland has the second highest proportion of Norwegian ancestry among the British Isles, next only to Orkney (though Shetland has not been so comprehensively analysed).[107] The period when Norwegian ancestry entered Ireland is presumed to be the Viking Age.

Not only settlements but also hoards witness to the presence of the Vikings. Around 135 hoards are known from Ireland, consisting of coins (included in seventy-one of the caches) and precious metals. The majority of hoards with non-numismatic material were deposited in the period ca. 850–950. Twenty-nine hoards which include ornaments alone have a noteworthy distribution: they are scattered around the country, mainly in areas outside Norse control such as in ring-forts, which indicates that objects were in the possession of indigenous people. Hoards with ingots are often found on ecclesiastical sites. Hack-silver (fragments of cut or bent silver used by weight as a currency) was a typical component of the Scandinavian bullion economy and this applied to Viking hoards in Ireland too.[108]

Rich monasteries were a focus of raiding and reliquaries were especially desired. Even more important to the Vikings were humans—slaves, particularly females, obliged to serve as concubines and domestics, rather than as labourers. Monasteries were frequently plundered by the Irish also, before, during, and after the ninth century, but they rarely destroyed holy relics.[109] As the authors of reports and chronicles, monks fairly or unfairly contributed to the Vikings' malign reputation.

From the beginning of the tenth century, Vikings began to engage in trade and they contributed to the expansion of commerce and the introduction of coinage. A potential *þing*-(thing) place, actually called Ting (south of Wexford), would suggest that the Vikings imported a key ingredient of their social system (the governing assembly), even if it was the only one of its kind in Ireland.[110]

Discoveries of burials in Cloghermore cave in southwest Ireland have contributed to the discussion regarding Viking conversion. Excavation revealed that Scandinavians continued to bury their dead there in accordance with Old Norse traditions as late as the end of the ninth and early tenth centuries.

After several set-backs, involving attacks from the native Irish, the first Viking occupation of Dublin ended in 902 and their rulers left for Scotland. A Norse presence remained in Dublin, albeit with a reduced population. The Norse rulers returned to Ireland in 914, when a great fleet arrived in Waterford, and in 917 settlement was re-established in Dublin and Hiberno-Scandinavian graves thenceforward re-appear. Dublin and York were now ruled by the same Scandinavian dynasty.[111] Viking military power ended in Ireland at the end of the tenth century, although influence persisted in the use of Old Norse loan words, like *stiúir* (rudder), and *mogadh* (market) and property boundaries in Dublin endured for centuries after their establishment.[112]

England

The raid on Portland, Dorset, in 789 is the first known in England. The pirates were described as "Northmen from Hordaland" (western Norway) and also "Danish men." The *Anglo-Saxon Chronicle* says that the royal reeve and his followers were killed. More famous is the attack on the church of Lindisfarne in 793, which some regard as marking the start of the Viking Age. In the words of the Northumbrian scholar Alcuin:

> Never before has such terror appeared in Britain as we have now suffered from a pagan race. [...] The heathens poured out the blood of saints around the altar, and trampled on the bodies of saints in the temple of God, like dung in the streets.[113]

Subsequent strikes on Northumbria took place in 794. The *Chronicle* is silent about more raids until 835, but it is known from other documents that intensive Viking activity took place in Kent where Norse camps were established from 792 to 822.[114]

Upon colonization, Scandinavians seem not to have cleared new land in England—they simply purloined existing farms and re-named them. While land was rarely owned individually in England before the ninth century, Viking leaders divided land and gave it as a reward for military service. This contributed to the division and re-allocation of plots and privatization. Not only Vikings bought land, so did English lords.[115]

From a Scandinavian perspective, the eventual colonization of a substantial portion of England must have been regarded as a success. It reached its apogee with the establishment of the Danelaw (*Dena lage*),[116] an area ruled by Danish kings under Danish law from the early eleventh century. This was an extensive territory which the Danes had managed to colonize and over which they had exercised some

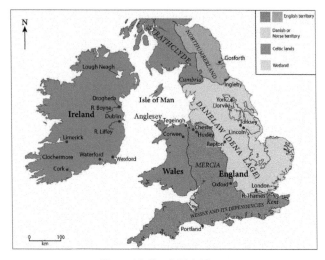

Figure 18. The British Isles—
map with key names, including the Danelaw.

control since the ninth century, but its geographical area
seems to have varied in space and time (Figure 18). Scandinavian influence in the area of the Danelaw is displayed especially by place names, particularly names in *-by* and *-thorp*
that are found concentrated in Lincolnshire and Yorkshire.[117]
The extent of the legal reach and nature of the Danelaw as
a cultural and political unit with Scandinavian characteristics
has been questioned given that the Danish King Cnut aspired
to be a just, Christian king like those in England. There may
have been beneficial cultural encounters between Danes and
Anglo-Saxons as well as the converse.[118]

   The Norse are generally considered to have encouraged
the expansion of trade and urbanization in England, and to
have helped the development of towns such as York and
Lincoln. The causal relationship between the Vikings and
urbanization is, however, a matter of similar debate to that
in Ireland. Even if the urban centres in England increased

from a dozen trading places to more than a hundred towns in this period, including a large number of *wics*, urbanization may have been part of an existing process. The Vikings may have contributed indirectly to urbanization and exchange by expropriating land in rural areas. Former owners may have been forced to move to nascent urban centres to make a living, for instance by manufacture. Manufacturing underwent almost industrial-scale development in England during the Viking Age—was this stimulated by urbanization or the Scandinavian arrivals? In addition, a number of places (cf. *burhs*) were fortified or re-fortified as a consequence of the Viking raids, and some of these were regenerated as urban centres, particularly York, Chester, and Oxford.

Several sources suggest that the Vikings participated in various forms of exchange, not only robbery or extortion. In Scandinavia, trade in this period consisted of barter, with a frequent use of hack-silver and other commodities. Apart from possible mints in Ribe and Hedeby in the first half of the ninth century, more continuous minting in Scandinavia did not start before the 990s (Chapter 2).[119] Coins were introduced only towards the end of the Viking Age in Scandinavia and a bullion economy was clearly employed by the Norse in the British Isles. Viking Age hoards, including hack-silver and arm-rings, are found particularly in the north and northwest of England, with a growing body of material being revealed by metal detectorists. A typical example is the Huxley hoard from Cheshire dating to ca. 850–950, with twenty-two band-shaped penannular arm-rings comprising around 1.4 kg of silver; there is also the more varied and large hoard from the Vale of York, with ornaments, ingots, hack-silver, and more than six hundred coins dated to the 920s. Much silver was extorted from the local population to the Vikings as tribute (*Danegeld*). This was more profitable than robbery. Silver in the form of minted coins was paid as *Danegeld* to the Viking armies. Many mints in England are known only from the period of *Danegeld*, and their number decreased after this (Figure 19).[120]

It has been argued that Vikings engaged in trade when they over-wintered in camps. Several Viking camps are known,

Figure 19. Typical Viking silver hoard objects:
ingots, coins, silver arm-rings, and hack silver,
from Vale of York, England, early tenth century.

such as those in Kent on the Isles of Thanet and Sheppey
from 850 and 855 respectively. In the decade from 865, the
members of the Great Army (the gathering of Viking warriors
which moved out of York to maraud in Mercia and Wessex)
were transformed into settlers, ploughing fields and supporting themselves. One example of a winter camp turning into a
permanent settlement is Torksey in Lincolnshire, occupied in
872–73 and located strategically to the east of the River Trent
with access to rich resources.[121] Their bullion-based economy
comprising ingots, hack-silver, hack-gold, and hack-copper,
weights, Islamic coins, and traces of local coin production
are evidence of this. Apart from trading the produce of large-
scale plundering, and probably slaving and fishing, they were
craftworkers in textiles, wood, and metal. The example of
Torksey shows that the Vikings managed to build some type
of pragmatic relationship with the native population, even if
it was based on asymmetric power.

Norse dwellings of the longhouse type (see below) would
seem to be absent from England. This might foster the notion

that the colonisers adapted to local traditions, perhaps by having their dwellings constructed by indigenous artisans. Settlements with houses in which the Norse lived might best be demonstrated in towns with a significant Scandinavian population, such as York (*Jorvik*). There, houses were constructed in a post and wattle tradition (thin branches woven between upright stakes). They were rectangular, single storeyed, and with a central hearth and sometimes wattle-lined wall benches. Houses from the ninth to eleventh centuries in York are similar to those in the Norse settlements of Dublin and Waterford. This might argue for the idea that such houses were built in accordance with Scandinavian designs. Wattle-constructed walls are found in a town like Hedeby, as in other parts of Scandinavia (Chapter 2).

Some graves are easily identified by ritual and grave goods. For instance, a woman in her forties was buried in traditional Scandinavian costume in South Yorkshire in the late ninth century. Grave goods including a knife, a key, and a bowl, as well as isotopic analysis of her bones, suggested that she came from Norway.[122] Like houses, however, it can be difficult to determine if a grave is Scandinavian or not. Diverse burial customs among Anglo-Saxons as well as among the Norse make it hard to identify ethnicity. Furnished graves can be found in cemeteries, even with the remains of a boat, in otherwise Christian contexts. This means that the distinction between Christian and other burials may not be straightforward. We need to be careful and not use grave goods solely as a criterion for non-Christian burials, but even so, some Scandinavian burials are identified, though not as frequently as might be expected. Fewer than twenty-five Old Norse burial sites have been identified in England from the ninth and tenth centuries (e.g., at Ingleby and Repton). These numbers are expected to increase in the future: four hundred and fifty items of Scandinavian-style jewellery, which amounts to 89 percent of the total corpus (up to 2008), were found by metal detectorists.[123]

England was Christian by the time that the Vikings arrived, and the Scandinavians seem to have undergone an early conversion. This could explain the low number of Old Norse burial sites. After settlement, the incomers may have regarded church construction as a means to enhance their status as good Christians. Vikings probably adopted more characteristics from the Anglo-Saxons than simply religion, including the incorporation of new designs and products which again hinders our ability to discriminate between the two groups. A mixture of styles and motifs is demonstrated on stone monuments, displaying a blend of Anglo-Saxon, Scandinavian, and Celtic traditions. The Gosforth Cross in Cumbria depicts what is interpreted as Old Norse and Christian mythology. The so-called "hogbacks" are another example—tombstones fashioned like a bow-shaped building, some with a beast at each end. They are not found in Scandinavia, with the exception of one from Norderhov, close to Oslo. Yet their Scandinavian affiliation is demonstrated by their longhouse-like design and their distribution in areas with Norse place names; but they appear to have originated in the north of England or the south of Scotland where the majority of hogbacks are found.[124]

If we turn to language and literature, only thirteen finds featuring runic inscriptions come from England. There is, however, a significant Scandinavian influence on legal terminology and even the word "law" is a loan word from Old Norse. This and other evidence may lead us to surmise a reasonable degree of mutual intelligibility between Norse- and English-speaking people in Viking Age England.[125] If so, this must have eased cultural encounters and the adoption of each other's ideas and words.

Wales

Norse raids to Wales are grouped in two phases. The first known raid is recorded in 852 and Anglesey was targeted specifically from 855. A second series of attacks on coastal areas started ca. 950.[126] This is perhaps unsurprising as Wales was centrally located for voyages between England, Ireland, the Isle of Man, and the Scottish isles. Place names and graves testify to the presence of Scandinavians especially in Welsh coastal areas and this is corroborated by eleven silver hoards with coins, arm-rings, and hack-silver, dating to the period 850–1030.[127]

From the second quarter of the tenth century we see a dramatic increase in sculptures, especially in coastal areas at Anglesey and Tegeingl (Englefield) that are known for their Hiberno-Scandinavian settlement. Here we find stone crosses influenced by Viking styles, perhaps in an effort to express ethnic identity.[128] The crosses are typically carved with a Borre-style interlaced ring-chain similar to other crosses around the Irish Sea. Stone sculpture in the rest of Wales was made in different styles, and they were probably initiated by the patronage of mother churches through ruling families.

Only one runic inscription (from Corwen, Merioneth) is found on stone sculptures in Wales, on a cross shaft. It has not been determined whether this inscription, thought to be read as "iþfus," is Scandinavian or Anglo-Saxon and the date is estimated as tenth or eleventh century.[129] The interpretation of the Welsh evidence would suggest that the area's Hiberno-Scandinavian settlers, at least in part, identified themselves as Christian at this time and had adopted local traditions such as stone sculpture production.

Isle of Man

The Isle of Man, sitting in the Irish Sea, was an important stepping stone for Scandinavian settlements around adjacent coastal areas, and it formed the southernmost of the "Southern islands" (Old Norse: *Suðreyar*) (Figure 20). Vikings settled the island in the late ninth and early tenth centuries, but many may have arrived from Ireland, not directly from Scandinavia, and they presumably converted to Christianity at an early stage. A male boat grave with weapons in a Christian cemetery at Balladoole is dated to this period, and the Norse influence on stone crosses and cross slabs is acknowledged.[130] The Scandinavians consolidated their settlement on Man in the early 900s when the first Norse-influenced crosses were produced. A number of these have inscriptions, both

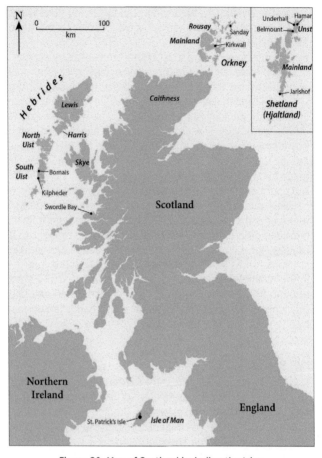

Figure 20. Map of Scotland including the Isles.

in ogham (a primarily early Irish script) and runic alphabets, reflecting probable cultural integration and intermarriages. Kermode lists twenty-six inscriptions with runes. Of forty-two personal names, twenty-eight are Scandinavian male and female names. The inscriptions list both genders as rune carvers and sculptors. Nowhere else in the Viking diaspora than on this small island do we find so many runic inscriptions from the Viking Age: thirty-three inscriptions in total, including inscriptions on crosses and other objects, compared to the thirteen from the whole of England.[131]

The dominance of male graves on the Isle of Man suggests that few Scandinavian women took part in the island's colonization. Intermarriages may have speeded up an acculturation process, as demonstrated by Christian conversions within a century of the Scandinavian arrivals. Intermarriage between Norse and local population seems like a natural and necessary solution to build a new family structure, if there was to be a permanent settlement for the Scandinavians: of around forty Scandinavian graves, only one included the burial of both a man and woman; all the others were male. The males would need to look for spouses as soon as settlement was underway. Y–chromosone DNA suggests that 25 percent of the modern male population were of "North European/Scandinavian" origin and 65 percent "could be deemed to be of Celtic origin." Nine of 105 Manx families tested descend from a single man of likely Scandinavian background.[132]

Christianity had been established on Man during the sixth century, long before the Vikings arrived. The early Christian Church was centred on the tidal St Patrick's Isle. This continued to be the centre for the see of the Isle of Man and the Hebrides which was made a suffragan bishopric under the Norwegian archdiocese of Nidaros in the mid-1100s and stayed as such until 1472.[133] In the thirteenth century, the Isle of Man became part of the kingdom of Norway, like the Norse areas in Scotland and the North Atlantic region. The fact that the Isle of Man and the Hebrides (within the *Suðreyar*) were subordinated to Nidaros in the middle of the twelfth century would have been unthinkable without substantial Norse influence during the Viking Age.

The Isle of Man parliament—Tynwald (Manx: *Tinvaal*)—is probably a *-thing* place and claims to be the oldest continuously operating legislature in the world. As such, it would reinforce the evidence for Scandinavian influence or authority.

Scotland

The Scandinavian immigration to Scotland took place primarily in the Northern and Western Isles, but it embraced neighbouring coastal areas and especially Caithness. Settlement had likely begun in Shetland and Orkney during the early ninth century. Apart from Norse place names, graves, houses, hoards, and stray finds, the Orkney boat burials on Rousay and Sanday show Scandinavian influence. The latter included grave goods which indicate that the Norse were continuing their farming, fishing, and warrior traditions.

House remains on Shetland prove the importance of the Vikings' traditional longhouse type, imported to Scotland. Those on Unst are the best known, with more than sixty possible longhouse sites of which Belmont, Hamar, and Upper Underhoull were recently excavated (Figure 21).[134] At Jarlshof on Mainland, Shetland as well as Kilpheder and Bornais on South Uist in the Outer Hebrides, the longhouses are located in the midst of prehistoric dwellings. The Norse builders do not appear to have re-used former structures, although they may have taken advantage of the readily available stone. The Norse longhouse offered a familiar domestic space to the incomers which may reflect stronger power relationships in Scotland than was to be found in England and Ireland where local building styles were adopted by the Scandinavians (see above).

There is a near-total dominance of Norse place names in Shetland and Orkney with just a minority remaining from Pictish, Celtic, and English. Place-name evidence might be assumed to reflect the near-total takeover, perhaps even genocide (albeit that is contested), of the indigenous popu-

Figure 21. A Norse longhouse at Belmont, Unst, Shetland, Scotland.

lation.[135] The Norse dominance could be reflected in the Irish title of *Innse Gall* ("Islands of the Foreigners") for the Outer Hebrides.[136] The situation in the Western Isles is complicated by the fact that there is a post-Scandinavian Gaelic overlay of place names, including admixtures of Norse and Gaelic names. Lest it be thought that Old Norse onomastics applies in all its aspects to the islands and the rest of Scotland, it might be noted that place names with sacral connotations (like *helga*, holy, and *hof*, cult building), are rarely found. However, in both the archipelagos of the Northern and Western Isles, pre-Norse place names seem not to have survived other than possibly for a few island names such as Unst, Fetlar, Yell, Lewis, and the Uists.

Fewer Viking archaeological sites are known from mainland Scotland. Most graves are found to the far north, a distribution supported by the general spread of hoards and runic inscriptions. The first complete Scandinavian boat burial on the UK mainland, dating from the late ninth/early tenth century, was found as recently as 2011 in Swordle Bay, Ard-namurchan, adjacent to the Atlantic seaways.[137]

Scotland is the only region in the Viking diaspora which can compete with the Isle of Man with respect to the number of runic inscriptions from the Viking Age: thirty are located in Scotland, but twenty-three of these are from Orkney and Shetland, compared with the thirty-three on Man.[138]

DNA analyses of modern populations suggest that Scandinavian immigrants to the Northern and Western Isles exceed the numbers with a Norse genetic profile from mainland Britain. The genetic evidence also indicates that more of the immigrants were male than female. This may be supported by the evidence from furnished graves: of 379 proposed Viking graves, two hundred contained weapons, and graves with weapons outnumber graves with female objects.[139]

The close relationship between the Scottish isles especially and Norway, from the Viking Age and through much of the Middle Ages, is bolstered by the fact that these parts of Scotland were subordinate to the Archbishopric of Nidaros in the mid-1150s, with a bishop's seat at Kirkwall. Orkney remained a suffragan bishopric under Nidaros until 1472.

The North Atlantic

The Vikings turned their attention to the North Atlantic region from at least 800. Their colonization involved long sea journeys stretching beyond Scotland to Newfoundland and embracing the Faroe Islands, Iceland, and Greenland. The impetus for these extended, dangerous travels may be found in a number of areas, many of which are inter-related (see Chapter 4). Population pressures and political disharmony in Norway, for instance, encouraged settlers to seek new lands further afield. The British Isles fulfilled needs to a certain extent, but exploring more distant pristine territories would have been less trouble (in terms of conflict) and at least as exciting. Although the initial attraction might have been land, economic considerations (including the desire for marketable goods such as ivory, furs, and falcons) also came into play, certainly as far as Greenland was concerned.

The length of the sea voyages and navigational details are outlined in the Icelandic *Landnámabók* (Book of Settlements) of the twelfth or thirteenth centuries (Figure 22). For the journey from Hernar (south of Stad) in Norway to Hvarv in Greenland, the seaman is told to:

> Sail north of Shetland, so that it can be seen if visibility is good; south of the Faroe Islands so that the sea's horizon is level with the middle of the mountain sides; and so far south of Iceland that birds and whales are in evidence.[140]

The *landnám* (from Old Norse and meaning "land taking") refers to the initial settlement of the North Atlantic islands and is often used to denote the clearance of scrub and woodland for agriculture, especially in Iceland and Greenland. [141] The Faroe Islands were not substantially wooded at the time of *landnám*.

Environmental conditions in the North Atlantic were generally much harsher than were to be found in the Viking homelands. Soils were often thinner, highly minerogenic, and waterlogged; Icelandic landscapes were subject to lava flows, volcanic eruptions, and *jökulhlaups* (glacial outburst floods); the available land in Greenland was restricted severely by ice and snow cover, while seasonal pack-ice limited access to coastal areas and sea-borne communication beyond the islands. Once *landnám* was underway, the woodland resource became much depleted and the demand for building and heating materials meant that alternatives were required. Turf and stone buildings and farm structures and walls were the norm, heating was supplied by peat and driftwood, with light coming from hearths and oil lamps.[142]

The Irish monk Dicuil, writing at the Frankish Court around 825, talks of a group of islands two days sailing north of the British Isles that were occupied by anchorites (*papar*) before they were ejected by "Northman pirates" (Text Box 3). This has been widely assumed to refer to an Irish priestly presence on the Faroe Islands before the arrival of the Vikings. Similar claims have been made for Iceland. These possibilities are discussed below. The area of southern Greenland occupied

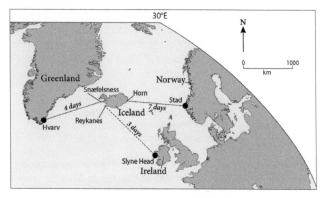

Figure 22. North Atlantic voyage times
as outlined in *Landnámabok*.

by the Norse was empty of people at the time of their arrival, but coastal areas were utilized seasonally by Thule Culture hunter-fishers during the post-Viking Age (ca. 1350–1450, and still within the Norse period. The Labrador mainland was populated by Beothuk "Indians" at the time of the Norse arrival in Newfoundland.

The Faroe Islands

The eighteen islands of the Faroes (*Føroyar*, "sheep islands") are essentially basalt slabs rising sharply from the sea (Figure 23). Only 5 percent of the land surface is cultivated today and it would have been less during the Viking era. The dominant vegetation is sedge-heath grassland, and woodland in the form of low shrubby flora has always been of minor importance. While suitable for grazing in both infields and outfields, the Faroese landscape is ill-suited to extensive cereal cultivation. Peat and driftwood were exploited for building materials and heating.[143] Fishing, seabirds, and marine mammals were a vital supplement to food resources. Birds provided feathers, eggs, and, from fulmars, possibly oil for lamps.

Dicuil's statements on the *papar* received an impetus with the discovery of burnt peat layers containing carbonized barley grains at Á Sondum on Sandoy. The grain was radiocarbon-dated to two phases of activity some three to five hundred years prior to 800, the assumed arrival date of the Vikings in the Faroe Islands. These deposits are overlain by a longhouse dating to the ninth century. It is not possible to say which pre-Viking peoples were responsible for the grain, but the evidence does show the presence of people before the conventional arrival date of the Norse. The existence of supposed ancient field systems at locations such as Lambi (Mykines), Akraberg (Suðuroy) and á Teigalendi beside Á Sondum, along with cereal-type pollen in pre-Norse contexts, and several place names indicating *papar*, have been adduced as further indications of a precocious human presence in the archipelago, but the dating evidence in these instances is uncertain.[144] Barley seems to have been grown from the beginning of Norse settlement, given the early dates (centred on ca. 800) for grain from Við Kirkjugard on Sandur (Figure 24).

The arrival of the Vikings at *landnám* may have been made easier by the survival of sheep from either the time of the *papar* or, conceivably, as happened in Iceland, the establishment of breeding pairs of sheep left on the islands by an advance party of Scandinavians hoping to build-up flocks. Settlement necessarily took place on the small areas of level land along the coast and fjords, and preparation of the land was aided by the lack of trees. Genetic evidence suggests that two-thirds of male colonisers may have been of Scandinavian origin while a similar proportion of the women may have come from the British Isles, presumably used as slaves and concubines, if not wives.

Viking Age longhouses made variously of stone, turf, and timber have been excavated, most notably at Kvívík on Streymoy and Toftanes on Eysturoy. In addition, research has taken place on the shieling site complex at Argisbrekka, Eysturoy. Toftanes produced an extensive suite of artefacts including querns, steatite objects, spindle whorls, whetstones, wooden

Figure 23. Map of Iceland and the Faroe Islands.

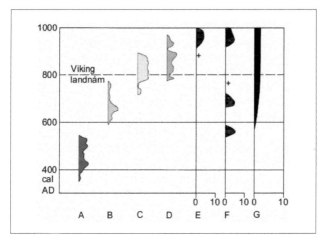

Figure 24. Palaeoenvironmental and archaeological data associated with Á Sondum, Sandoy, Faroe Islands. Calibrated radiocarbon dates for archaeological contexts from Á Sondum compared to the time of appearance of peat ash patches (A, B); longhouse external midden (C) and central hearth (D); barley (*Hordeum*) type pollen percentages from the sites of Hov (E, F) and Heimavatn (G).

barrel staves, bowls, spoons, and crosses (the latter made from driftwood). Of particular interest at Toftanes were the boulders entwined with juniper cords which were probably used as roofing stones, two ringed pins of Hiberno-Norse type, and a jet bracelet.[145] Grave sites are relatively rare, but Norse burials have been inferred at Tjørnuvík and at Sandur which also possesses a fine Christian cemetery associated with the earliest of its six churches. Christianity supposedly arrived ca. 1000—it is a moot point whether the circular prayer-house sites (*bønhús*) are of earlier Hiberno-Scandinavian origin.[146]

Coastal sites had infields where hay and some barley were grown and shieling areas, denoted by *ærgi* and *sel* place names and several archaeological structures, beyond the set-tlements.[147] The shielings were replaced later by more exten-sive grazed outfields (*hagi*) and locales for peat extraction (for fuel and building material, as turf). Sheep predominated over cattle, pigs, and goats, although the remains of birds (espe-cially puffin and guillemot), fish (especially Atlantic cod), and shellfish (e.g., limpets, although these are as likely to have been bait for fishing as human food) are collectively more abundant than domesticated animals. Whale and seal were also eaten. The human diet has been estimated as being 20 to 40 percent marine on the basis of skeletal isotope analysis.

Iceland

It is fortunate that the deposition of a volcanic tephra layer in Iceland marks more or less precisely the beginning of the set-tlement period (Figure 23). This so-called "*landnám* tephra" layer, dated to 871±2, corresponds closely with the formation of the many farmsteads which it underlays. There are also several sites in western Iceland which immediately precede ash deposition, as well as pollen sites displaying cereal-type pollen just beneath the *landnám* tephra, but these do not constitute the norm. There is a suggestion in Dicuil's writ-ings that the priestly *papar* reached "Thule," which may be equated with Iceland, and before this, the fantastical *Navi-gatio Sancti Brendani Abbatis* (Voyage of Saint Brendan the Abbot) spoke of a land of ice and fire. Iceland, like the Faroes, possesses *papar* place names, most notably the island of Papey off Iceland's east coast.

The *Landnámabók* details the establishment of some four-teen hundred settlements, together with the names of more than three thousand settlers. Many of the settlements are known, but it is a severe under-representation of the total, and the intention of the text in part may have been to jus-tify land claims and the status of several hundred import-ant founding settlers (*landnámsmen*). A strongly contested re-assessment of the peopling of Iceland argues that a mini-mum of twenty-four thousand people must have been transported to Iceland in less than twenty years to account for the dates and density of sites in the Mývatn area of northeast Iceland.[148]

Landnámabók also tells that many of the settlers, predominantly male, came from Norway and others from the Irish Sea area. Although the colonisers might be thought to be solidly Norse, DNA from modern Icelanders suggests that men (75 percent) came dominantly from Scandinavia and women (62 percent) from the British Isles—in line with earlier observations on blood groups and folk lore.[149] Once again, an accepted interpretation is that male Vikings took British and Irish women as slaves or wives. A study of ancient genomes confirms Norse, Gaelic, and intermixed individuals, but that genetic drift in modern populations has likely been influenced by later immigration from Denmark which maintained colonial control over Iceland from the late fourteenth century to 1944.[150] The ancient DNA investigation makes the observation that reproductive success among the earliest Icelanders was possibly stratified by ancestry, with many slaves amongst the Gaelic settlers for whom survival and freedom to reproduce was likely to have been constrained.

The ethnic mix is perhaps indicated by burials, all of which were inhumations except for one possible cremation (Hrísbrú), thus being more akin to practice in the British Isles than to Scandinavia where cremation was common in many areas. Viking Age graves in Iceland are often found either just outside homefields, or further away, out of sight of the settlement and close to farm boundaries. They are liminal, frequently associated with routeways, but almost every farm had its own burial ground. This is in contrast to Christian cemeteries, whose numbers were far fewer and would seem to promote centrality in burying. The non-Christian burial customs stopped around 1000, when Christian burial rituals took over.[151]

According to the twelfth-century *Íslendingabók* (Book of the Icelanders), woodland at the time of *landnám* stretched from the mountains to the seashore. Pollen-analytical research shows this to be an exaggeration, but the initial colonisers were greeted by an extensive tree birch cover when they arrived. This was rapidly removed, by axe as well as fire, in an effort to create open space for farms and pastures; it should be noted that in some areas the birch woodland was already decreasing probably as a result of climate change. While peat may have eventually replaced wood for most domestic heating, taxa such as birch and willow were used for charcoal production and iron smelting, necessitating woodland management (including coppicing). The depletion of the woodland resource seems to have been widespread elsewhere and this, along with the trampling of grazing animals, led to extensive soil erosion evident in sediment profiles from *landnám* onwards (Figure 25).[152]

Scholars are not certain about how settlement spread, but one model holds that coastal locations were occupied first prior to expanding inland, even as far as interior rangelands and sometimes highlands. It is assumed that the inferior locations were settled by the later or less powerful immigrants. The most successful initial settlers were often seen as chieftains (*goðor*) who were able to allocate areas of land to their followers. Excavations demonstrate the antiquity (near-*landnám*) of many farms (e.g., Stöng, Hrísbrú, and Hofstaðir) as well as their relative size and wealth. Evidence from Hrísbrú suggests that beef and beer were served at feasts. This would have required both the cultivation and acquisition of barley. Over time, this cultivation moved towards the coast, probably for climatic reasons (Figure 26).[153]

Research has shown that if appropriate science-based interdisciplinary teams, investigating multiple sites, are deployed over extensive areas rather than effort being concentrated on a single prestige site and its immediate catchment area, then results can confound established narratives.[154] Thus, for Mývatnssveit, inland settlement was early and extensive, possibly involving whole communities. We can observe localized rather than widespread woodland clearance, woodland management then taking place, and severe soil erosion came much later than *landnám*. The reduction in pigs and goats may reflect efforts to inhibit woodland destruction rather than

Figure 25. Peat section near Hrísbrú, Mosfell, Iceland.
The pre-Norse sedge-wood deposits show that woodland was
diminished at the time of deposition of the landnám volcanic
tephra and the appearance of anthropogenic pollen indicators
(e.g., from cereal cultivation). The lighter coloured silty peat
has an admixture of wind-blown and slopewash materials
resulting in part from farm-based soil erosion.

being a response to deforestation. Pre-Christian socio-polit-
ical organization was complex, embracing the exchange of
staple goods, charcoal and iron production, and ritual feasting
based on cattle at the farm of Hofstaðir—indeed, eleven cattle
skulls, apparently display items given the skeletal weathering
patterns, were found in the terminal floor layers of the hall.
Trade and connectivity are demonstrated by the presence of
eggshells, cod, seal, porpoise and seabird bones up to sixty
kilometres from the nearest coastal areas.

A central assembly place for Iceland, the Althing, was
established ca. 930 at Thingvellir. Christianity was mandated

Figure 26. A reconstructed Norse house at Eirikstaðir, Iceland.

for Iceland at the Althing in 999 or 1000, although the population as a whole did not instantly change religion and jettison all its traditions. From this time on, however, non-Christian graves disappeared abruptly, and some private churches and Christian cemeteries are to be found dating from the eleventh century. The cemetery at Keldudalur may even contain graves older than 1000.[155] In spite of public conversion, Icelanders agreed to maintain several Norse traditions in opposition to Christian practice, such as the eating of horse meat and infanticide, at least until 1016. The Christianization of Iceland ultimately involved two bishoprics, at Skálholt and Hólar, coming under the Nidaros see when it was founded in Norway in 1153.

Greenland

According to *Grænlendinga saga* (Saga of the Greenlanders), the colonization of Greenland began with the exile of *Eiríkr rauði* (Erik the Red) from Iceland following his conviction for manslaughter around 982. This was something of a family tradition—his father, Thorvald Ásvaldsson from Jæren in Norway, had also been banished following a conviction for manslaughter and had voyaged to Iceland. Erik spent three years as an outcast exploring coastal southwestern Greenland, an area which is snow and ice-free during the summer at least. The existence of Greenland was already known and may already have experienced attempted colonization, but it was Erik who returned to Iceland and sold the idea of settlement to impoverished Icelanders, aided by the somewhat misleading name of *Green*land. *Landnámabók* states that twenty-five ships left for Greenland in ca. 985, bringing horses, other farm animals, and wives. Even if climatic conditions during the so-called "Medieval Warm Period" around 950–1250 were conducive to North Atlantic voyaging, average conditions do not signify constantly benign ones. Only fourteen vessels arrived safely and eleven were lost by the time that Erik's entourage rounded Cape Farewell. Erik settled in the fertile inlet of what was to become Eiríksfjörðr, occupying the site of *Brattahlið* (popularly assumed to be present-day Qassiarsuk) which had presumably been earmarked by him during his exile.

Colonization proceeded across two principal areas known as The Eastern (Old Norse: *Eystribyggð*) and Western Settlements (Old Norse: *Vestribyggð*) (Figure 27). The Eastern Settlement is in the extreme south of Greenland, a sea journey of some six hundred kilometres from its "western" partner. The former was a more extensive area containing about two hundred and fifty to three hundred farms (what constitutes a farm can be difficult to determine and not all "ruin groups" were contemporaneous). The Eastern Settlement had a more attractive climate for agriculture and it was closer to the sea lanes of Iceland and Europe.[156] In contrast, the Western Settlement, consisting of around sixty to ninety farms, placed greater reliance on the hunting of animals on both land and sea as a means of subsistence, though animal husbandry was still important.[157] The so-called Middle Settlement (a modern construct; Danish: *Mellembygden*) is generally seen as an extension of the Eastern Settlement from which it is physically separated, around 135 nautical miles (250 km) from the *Eystribyggð*, even if it is only sixty kilometres as measured

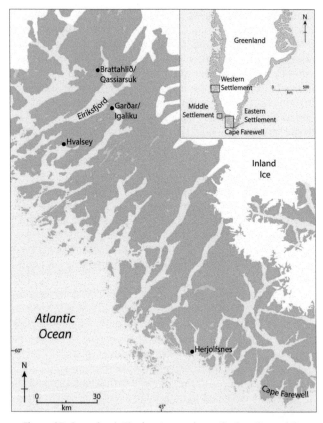

Figure 27. Greenland. The inset map shows the locations of the main clusters of dwellings: the Eastern (Eystribyggð), Middle and Western (Vestribyggð) Settlements. The main map shows some key ruin group/farm locations in the Eastern Settlement.

by straight-line distance. The area has received relatively little attention.[158] Its Norse components consist of at least forty-one known sites, twenty of which have less than five associated ruins. The coastal location of farms in *Mellembygden* distinguishes it from the other settlement areas (which can extend some hundred kilometres from the coast to the inland ice cap). It has more in common topographically with the Western Settlement, as the steepness of the mountains and hillslopes and their close proximity to the coast limit the availability of agricultural land. Furthermore, the shallowness of the soils would have prohibited the development of extensive homefields. In spite of the large number of farms in Norse Greenland, they were not all in occupation throughout the Norse period, and one estimate suggests a population rising from five hundred people at the start of settlement to two thousand around the end of the Viking period (Figure 28).[159]

Vegetation in coastal areas, especially away from exposed coasts, was characterized by widespread birch and willow scrub which had to be at least partly cleared before pastoralism could begin. It is evident from a number of pollen-related sedimentary sequences that scrub clearance was accompanied by soil erosion—the imposition of European agriculture upon pristine landscapes was often too much for fragile ecosystems.

The Norse economy was dependent on a combination of animal husbandry and exploitation of marine resources along with the hunting of native caribou (reindeer). Cattle, sheep, and goats were likely valued for such dairy products as milk, butter, and cheese. The over-wintering of cattle necessitated the collection and storage of fodder, hence the importance of homefields and pasture. Nevertheless, desiccating winds blowing from the inland ice caps would have hindered grass yields. A number of sites, most notably that of the cathedral farm of *Garðar* (Igaliku), display strong evidence for systems of irrigation channels, dams, and reservoirs.[160] The need for irrigation as part of the farming strategy in Greenland is thought to be a response to factors such as water shortage, soil nutrient loss, and the need to increase hay yields. A

Figure 28. Landscape and ruin group from Hvalsey Fjord in the Eastern Settlement, showing the church (thirteenth century) and the adjacent ruin group which may date originally from the early Norse settlement of Greenland.

question arises as to whether the irrigation technology was imported from Norway with the bishop in ca. 1126, or did it grow out of practices already under development in Viking Age Greenland?[161]

There is a small amount of evidence from plant macro-fossils and pollen that cereals (barley) were cultivated, but this would have been a minor activity; we are also told in the thirteenth-century *Konungs skuggsjá* ("King's Mirror") that bread was unknown in Greenland. A dependence on marine resources is shown by the frequent dominance of seal bone, especially from the migratory hooded and harp seals, in archaeozoological assemblages recovered during excavations in the Eastern and Western Settlements respectively. Stable isotope evidence suggests that marine foods became more important over time.[162]

Survival of the Greenlandic colony supposedly depended upon the import of iron and some timber from Europe, in return for exports such as seal skins, walrus hide ropes, walrus tusks for ivory products, narwhal tusks, and polar bear furs. Some of these products were obtained on hunting trips to the *Norðrsetur*, the northern hunting grounds, far to the north of the Western Settlement. The key economic importance of Greenlandic walrus ivory to this activity is a topic of considerable debate,[163] and recent ancient DNA analyses have led some researchers to query whether walrus ivory really was a primary motive for the settlement of Greenland.[164]

It has long been suggested that the Greenlandic Norse lived in stone and turf longhouses, often with a core of wooden panels, as well as in more complex passage houses which are assumed to represent a later adaptation to colder conditions whereby dwellings may contain large numbers of rooms and even byres. This view has been questioned[165] and it is now proposed that in addition to longhouses there were also "row houses" with attached rooms. This view argues that houses with a simple passage were rare, they often contain no central passage, and so are better described as centralized "conglomerate" buildings containing a large number of rooms and even byres (e.g., the Western Settlement farms V53d in Austmannedal, with its possible twenty-three rooms and no central passage, and Gården Under Sandet ("the farm beneath the sand") which comprised thirty-eight rooms). It is worth emphasizing that most houses are not firmly dated and it may be the case that types co-existed.

Twenty churches are known in Greenland, mostly in the Eastern Settlement, but with four in the Western and none in the Middle Settlement. Greenland's sole bishopric, associated with the cathedral at Garður (Igaliku) in the adjacent fjord to Eiríksfjörðr, dates to 1126, after the Viking Age.

Newfoundland

The furthest west that a proven Norse presence is to be found, and the only one in North America, is at the northwestern tip of Newfoundland (Figures 29 and 30). The archaeological site of L'Anse aux Meadows was discovered by Norwegian lawyer,

Figure 29. Map of Newfoundland and adjacent areas of eastern Canada.

Figure 30. L'Anse aux Meadows, Newfoundland, Canada—site of the only known Norse site in North America. The settlement was located on the crescent-shaped area in the centre-right of the photograph. A reconstruction is visible to the top left.

author, and adventurer Helge Ingstad. Saga evidence had led a number of researchers to focus on the general area of the Canadian seaboard west of Greenland and to Newfoundland, while local knowledge suggested that the eventual excavation site was of some antiquity. The older (and probably more reliable) of the two Greenland sagas, *Grænlendinga saga* (the other being the Saga of Erik the Red), tells how Erik's son Leifr Eiriksson (known as Leif the Lucky) led an expedition to *Vínland* ("land of wine" / "land of meadows"), an area already spotted by Bjarni Herjólfsson when blown off course during an earlier expedition. Leif landed initially in Helluland ("Flat-Rock Land"; presumed to be Baffin Island), then Markland ("Forest Land"; perhaps Labrador) and finally the more agreeable Vinland, a land of vines and grapes or meadows with self-sown wheat.

Helge Ingstad's wife, Anne Stine, led the 1960s excavations and uncovered a building complex including three multi-roomed houses and associated workshops strung linearly along a beach terrace around seventy metres from the current coast. Set apart from these and closer to the sea is a smithing complex and one of the houses also contained a smithy. The settlement has been dated by radiocarbon to around 980–1020, but it is thought that the period of occupation was much more narrowly constrained and possibly only a decade in duration.[166] The occupation layers and middens are sparse and there is an absence of graves. No byres or stables were found, although there was a suggestion of pig.[167] Seal and whale were eaten along with caribou, wolf, fox, bear, fish, and birds. The find of a spindle whorl presumably indicates the keeping of sheep and wool production and the climate would have enabled animals to graze outside in winter. Artefacts include a bronze pin, a stone spinning whorl, net sinkers, iron rivets and slag, and pieces of worked wood. Of note are the finds of butternut (white walnut; *Juglans cinerea*) for which the closest known habitats are in the Gulf of St. Lawrence and New Brunswick, some 700 nautical miles (ca. 1300 km) southwest of L'Anse aux Meadows. Wild grapes (riverbank grapes; *Vitis riparia*) are to be found somewhat closer (400 nautical miles; 740 km). The saga suggestion of self-sown wheat, if correct, may refer to swards of the strand grass American dune wild-rye (*Elymus mollis*)[168] which grows locally and extensively on the neighbouring mainland.

The houses were of wood and turf construction and clearly intended for year-round habitation. The presence of three houses rather than a single house is unusual and, along with the attendant finds, it may reflect accommodation for the crews of three ships and associated artisans. Location would appear to be the dominant factor in the choice of site. It is not sheltered and was likely positioned to provide access to, and surveillance of, the Strait of Belle Isle across to the mainland coast of Labrador.

There were no indigenous residents near L'Anse aux Meadows at the time of Norse occupation. Trading apparently took place with ancestors of the Beothuk and other groups on mainland sites and the sagas suggest that relations were not always friendly. In spite of the advantages afforded by timber and grapes, Vinland would seem to have been a step too far for the relatively small Norse population of Greenland, and its emotional connections were to the east rather than the west. After a few years the Vinland base was abandoned—perhaps reminiscent of what was later to happen in Greenland itself.

As we have seen, the end of the Norse sojourn at L'Anse aux Meadows was not the end of the Viking Age or of the Vikings, but it does represent the most westerly proven Scandinavian presence during the Norse diaspora. Our next and final chapter contains some general observations and a look at the Viking impact today.

Text Box 2: Ibn Faḍlān's description of the Rus

Ibn Faḍlān said: I also saw the Rūsiyyah. They had come to trade and had disembarked at the Itil River- I have never seen bodies as nearly perfect as theirs. As tall as palm trees, fair and reddish. [...] They carry axes, swords, and daggers and always have them to hand. [...] They are dark from the tips of their toes right up to their necks— trees, pictures, and the like.

Every woman wears a small box of iron, silver, brass, or gold, depending on her husband's financial worth and social standing, tied at her breasts. The box has a ring to which a knife is attached, also tied at her breasts. The women wear neck rings of gold and silver. [...] For every [...] ten thousand dirhams, he has a neck ring made for his wife. [...]

They are the filthiest of all God's creatures. They have no modesty when it comes to defecating or urinating and do not wash themselves when intercourse puts them in a state of ritual impurity. They do not even wash their hands after eating. Indeed, they are like roaming asses. They arrive, moor their boats by the Itil, and build large wooden houses on its banks. They share a house, in groups of ten and twenty, sometimes more, sometimes fewer. Each reclines on a couch. They are accompanied by beautiful female slaves for trade with the merchants. They have intercourse with their female slaves in full view of their companions. Sometimes they gather in a group and do this in front of each other. [...]

She (a slave girl) carries it (a basin) from one man to the next and goes around to everyone in the house. Every man blows his nose and spits in the basin, and then washes his face and hair. [...]

I was told that they set fire to their chieftains when they die. Sometimes they do more, so I was very keen to verify this. Then I learned of the death of an important man. They had placed him in his grave, with a roof raised over him, for ten days while they finished cutting and sewing his garments. When the deceased is poor, they build a small boat for him, place him inside and burn it. When he is rich, they collect his possessions and divide them into three portions. One-third goes to his household, one-third is spent on his funeral garments, and one-third is spent on the alcohol they drink the day his female slave kills herself and is cremated with her master. They are addicted to alcohol. They drink it night and day. [...]

When the man I just mentioned died, they said to his female slaves, "Who will die with him?" One said, "I will." [...] The female slave drank alcohol every day and sang merrily and cheerfully.

I arrived at the river where his boat was moored on the day the chief and the female slave were set on fire. I noticed that the boat had been beached and that it was supported by four *khadhank* props. These props were surrounded by what looked like huge structures of wood. [...] An aged woman whom they called the Angel of Death turned up. [...] They dressed him (the deceased) in trousers, leggings, boots, a tunic, and a silk caftan with gold buttons. They placed a peaked silk cap fringed with sable on his head. They carried him inside the yurt that was on the ship and rested him on a quilt, propping him up with the cushions. They placed the alcohol, fruit, and basil beside him. Then they placed bread, meat, and onions in front of him. They cut a dog in two and threw it onto the boat. They placed all his weaponry beside him. They made two horses gallop into a sweat, cut them into pieces with a sword, and threw the meat onto the boat. They cut two cows into pieces and threw them on board. Then they produced a cock and a hen, killed them, and put them on board too.

Meanwhile, the female slave who had expressed her wish to die came and went, entering one yurt after another. The owner of the yurt would have intercourse with her and say, "Tell your master that I have done this out of love for you." At the time of the Friday late afternoon prayer they brought the female slave to an object they had built that resembled a door-frame. She stood on the hands of the men and rose like the sun above the door-frame. [...] she said, 'Look, I see all my dead kindred, seated.' The third time she said, 'Look, I see my master, seated in the Garden. The Garden is beautiful and dark-green. He is with his men and his retainers. He summons me. Go to him.'" They took her to the boat and she removed both of her bracelets, handing them to the woman called the Angel of Death, the one who would kill her. [...] men entered the yurt. They all had intercourse with the female slave and then laid her beside her master. Two held her feet, two her hands. The crone called the Angel of Death placed a rope around her neck with the ends crossing one another and handed it to two of the men to pull on. She advanced with a broad-bladed dagger and began to thrust it in between her ribs, here and there, while the two men strangled her with the rope until she died.

The deceased's nearest male relative came forward. He picked up a piece of wood and set it alight. He was completely naked. [...] He set fire to the wooden structures under the boat. The people came forward with sticks and firewood. They each carried a lighted stick that they threw on top of the wood. The wood caught fire. Then the boat, the yurt, the dead man, the female slave, and everything else on board caught fire. A fearsome wind picked up. The flames grew higher and higher and blazed fiercely.

One of the Rūsiyyah was standing beside me. I heard him speaking to the interpreter who was with me. I asked him what he had said, and he replied, "He said, 'You Arabs, you are a lot of fools!'" "Why is that?" "Because you purposefully take your nearest and dearest and those you whom you hold in the highest esteem and put them in the ground, where they are eaten by vermin and worms. We, on the other hand, cremate them there and then, so that they enter the Garden on the spot." [...]

The Rūsiyyah then built a structure like a round hillock over the beached boat, and placed a large piece of *khadhank* in the middle. They wrote the man's name and the name of the king of the Rūsiyyah on it. Then they left.

Ibn Faḍlān said: It is one of the customs of the king of the Rūsiyyah to keep in his palace four hundred of his bravest comrades and most trusted companions beside him. They die when he dies and sacrifice themselves to protect him. [...]

Excerpts from James E. Montgomery, ed. and trans., "Ibn Faḍlān: Mission to the Volga," in *Two Arabic Travel Books: Accounts of China and India and Mission to the Volga*, ed. and trans. James E, Montgomery (New York: New York University Press, 2014), 241–53.

Text Box 3: Dicuil's observations on perhaps Iceland and the Faroe Islands

14. There are many other islands in the ocean to the north of Britain which can be reached from the northern islands of Britain in a direct voyage of two days and nights with sails filled with a continuously favourable wind. A devout priest told me that in two summer days and the intervening night he sailed in a two-benched boat and entered one of them.

15. There is another set of small islands, nearly all separated by narrow stretches of water; in these for nearly a hundred years hermits sailing from our country, Ireland, have lived. But just as they were always deserted from the beginning of the world, so now because of the Northman pirates they are emptied of anchorites, and filled with countless sheep and very many diverse kinds of sea-birds. I have never found these islands mentioned in the authorities.

Dicuili, Liber de mensura orbis terrae, ed. J. J. Tierney,
Scriptores Latini Hiberniae 6 (Dublin: Dublin Institute for
Advanced Studies, 1967), 75 and 77.

Notes

[81] Mary A. Valante, *The Vikings in Ireland: Settlement, Trade and Urbanization* (Dublin: Four Courts, 2008), 68.

[82] Clive Tolley, "Language in Viking Age Finland. An Overview," in *Fibula, Fabula, Fact*, ed. Ahola, 91–103; Joonas Ahola, Frog, and Jenni Lucenius, eds., *The Viking Age in Åland: Insights into Identity and Remnants of Culture*, Suomalaisen Tiedeakatemian Toimituksia Humaniora (Helsinki: Finnish Academy of Science and Letters, 2014), 7–35.

[83] Torsten Edgren, "The Viking Age in Finland," in *The Viking World*, ed. Brink, 470–84; Lassi Heininen, Joonas Ahola, and Frog, "'Geopolitics' of the Viking Age?," in *Fibula, Fabula, Fact*, ed. Ahola, 296–320.

[84] Heiki Valk, "The Vikings and the Eastern Baltic," in The Viking World, ed. Brink, 485–96; Heininen, Ahola, and Frog, "'Geopolitics' of the Viking Age?"

[85] Androshchuk, *Vikings in the East*, 11.

[86] Hraundal, "New Perspectives on Eastern Vikings/Rus in Arabic Sources."

87 Duczko, *Viking Rus*, 253–54.

88 Thomas S. Noonan, "Scandinavians in European Russia," in *The Oxford Illustrated History of the Vikings*, ed. Peter Sawyer (Oxford: Oxford University Press, 2001), 134–55; Androshchuk 2013, pp. 3, 11.

89 Duczko, *Viking Rus*, 109.

90 Androshchuk, *Vikings in the East*, 161–62.

91 Duczko, *Viking Rus*, 132–33 and 252.

92 T. Douglas Price et al., "Isotopic Provenancing of the Salme Ship Burials."

93 Fjodor Androshchuk, "The Vikings in the East," in *The Viking World*, ed. Brink, 517–42; Androshchuk, *Vikings in the East*, 14–15; Leszek Gardela, *Scandinavian Amulets in Viking Age Poland*, Collectio Archaeologica Ressoviensis 33 (Rzeszów: Oficyna Wydwnicza "Zimowit," 2014), 20–25.

94 Duczko, *Viking Rus*, 257

95 Bagge, *From Viking Stronghold to Christian Kingdom*, 34, 126; Hraundal, "The Rus in Arabic Sources," 190.

96 Valeri Yotov, "Traces of the Presence of Scandinavian Warriors in the Balkans," in *Byzantium and the Viking World*, ed. Fedir Androshchuk, Jonathan Shepard, and Monica White, Acta Universitatis Upsaliensis Studia Byzantina Upsaliensia (Uppsala: Uppsala Universitet, 2016), 241–53.

97 Ann Christys, *Vikings in the South: Voyages to Iberia and the Mediterranean. Studies in Early Medieval History* (London: Bloomsbury, 2015), 95.

98 Christys, *Vikings in the South*.

99 Janet L. Nelson, "The Frankish Empire," in *The Oxford Illustrated History of the Vikings*, ed. Peter Sawyer (Oxford: Oxford University Press, 1997), 19–47 at 29.

100 Stephen M. Lewis, "Salt and the Earliest Scandinavian Raids in France: Was There a Connection?," *Viking and Medieval Scandinavia* 12 (2016): 103–36.

101 Roesdahl, *Viking og Hvidekrist*, 322.

102 Jean Renaud, "The Duchy of Normandy," in *The Viking World*, ed. Brink, 453–57.

103 Nelson, "The Frankish Empire."

104 Peter Sawyer, "The Age of the Vikings, and Before," in *The Oxford Illustrated History of the Vikings*, ed. Peter Sawyer (Oxford Oxford University Press, 2001), 1–18.

105 Niels Bonde and Frans-Arne Stylegar, "Roskilde 6—Et langskib fra Norge. Proveniens og alder," *Kuml (2011): 247–60.*

[106] Valante, *The Vikings in Ireland*, 37–50; Donnchadh Ó Corráin, "The Vikings and Ireland," in *The Viking World*, ed. Brink, 428–33.

[107] Stephen Leslie et al., "The Fine-Scale Genetic Structure of the British Population," *Nature* 519 (2015): 309–14; Edmund Gilbert et al., "The Irish DNA Atlas: Revealing Fine-Scale Population Structure and History within Irleand," *Nature: Scientific Reports* 7, no. 17199 (2017): 1–11. http://dx.doi.org/10.1038/s41598-017-17124-4.

[108] John Sheehan, "Viking-Age Hoards in Scotland and Ireland: Regional Diversities," in *Viking and Norse in the North Atlantic: Select Papers from the Proceedings of the Fourteenth Viking Congress Tórshavn, 19–30 July 2001*, ed. Andras Mortensen and Símun V. Arge (Tórshavn: Føroya, 2005), 323–28; John Sheehan, "Scoto-Scandinavian 'Ring-Money' and Ireland," in *Shetland and the Viking World: Papers from the Seventeenth Viking Congress, Lerwick*, ed. Val E. Turner, Olwyn A. Owen, and Doreen J. Waugh (Lerwick: Shetland Heritage, 2016), 271–77.

[109] Edward Culleton, *Celtic and Early Christian Wexford. AD 400 to 1166* (Dublin: Four Courts, 1999), 163–68; Valante, *The Vikings in Ireland*, 80–87.

[110] Culleton, *Celtic and Early Christian Wexford*, 168.

[111] Clare Downham, *Viking Kings of Britain and Ireland: The Dynasty of Ívarr to A.D. 1014* (Edinburgh: Dunedin Academic, 2007); Linzi Simpson, "The First Phase of Viking Activity in Ireland: Achaeological Evidence from Dublin," in *The Viking Age. Ireland and the West: Papers from the Proceedings of the Fifteenth Viking Congress, Cork, 18–27 August 2005*, ed. John Sheehan and Donnchadh Ó Corráin (Dublin: Four Courts Press, 2010), 418–29; Ó Corráin, "The Vikings and Ireland," 428–33.

[112] Rebecca Boyd, "Building Fences in Viking Dublin: Exploring Ireland's First Urban Community," in *Heritage, Diaspora and the Consumption of Culture: Movements in Irish Landscapes*, ed. Diane Sabenacio Nititham and Rebecca Boyd, Studies in Migration and Diaspora (London: Routledge, 2014), 11–26.

[113] Richards, *Viking Age England*, 30.

[114] Clare Downham, "Vikings in England," in *The Viking World*, ed. Brink, 342.

[115] Richards, *Viking Age England*, 51–72.

[116] Lesley Abrams, "Edward the Elder's Danelaw," in *Edward the Elder 899–924*, ed. N. J. Higham and D. H. Hill (Abingdon: Routledge, 2001), 128.

[117] Eric Christiansen, *The Norsemen in the Viking Age*, The Peoples of Europe (Oxford: Blackwell, 2006), 228; Gillian Fellows-Jensen,

"Scandinavian Place Names in the British Isles," in *The Viking World*, ed. Brink, 392–400.

[118] Katherine Holman, "Defining the Danelaw," in *Vikings and the Danelaw. Select Papers from the Proceedings of the Thirteenth Viking Congress, Nottingham and York, 21–30 August 1997*, ed. James Graham-Campbell et al. (Oxford: Oxbow Books, 2001), 1–11 at 2–8.

[119] See Chapter 2, Towns and Trade. We are informed that a hoard of 248 early ninth-century coins was found in Ribe, in October 2018, which may throw new light on this topic.

[120] James Graham-Campbell and Robert Philpott, eds., *The Huxley Viking Hoard. Scandinavian Settlement in the North West* (Liverpool: National Museums Liverpool, 2009); John Schofield and Alan Vince, *Medieval Towns: The Archaeology of British Towns in Their European Setting*, Studies in the Archaeology of Medieval Europe (London: Equinox, 2009), 157.

[121] Dawn M. Hadley and Julian D. Richards, "The Winter Camp of the Viking Great Army, AD 872–3, Torksey, Lincolnshire," *The Antiquaries Journal* 96 (2016): 23–67.

[122] Jane F. Kershaw, *Viking Identities. Scandinavian Jewellery in England*, Medieval History and Archaeology (Oxford: Oxford University Press, 2013), 157.

[123] Kershaw, *Viking Identities*, 11–12.

[124] Richards, *Viking Age England*, 182–188, 213–221.

[125] Holman, "Defining the Danelaw"; Matthew Townend, *Language and History in Viking Age England. Linguistic Relations Between Speakers of Old Norse and Old English*, Studies in the Early Middle Ages 6 (Turnhout: Brepols, 2002), 182–83; Jesch, *The Viking Diaspora*, 171.

[126] Mark Redknap, "The Vikings in Wales," in *The Viking World*, ed. Brink, 401–10.

[127] Redknap, "The Vikings in Wales."

[128] Nancy Edwards, "The Early Medieval Sculpture of North Wales: Context, Wealth and Patronage," in *Making Histories: Proceedings of the Sixth International Conference on Insular Art, York 2011*, ed. Jane Hawkes (Donington: Tyas, 2013), 50–64.

[129] Nancy Edwards, *A Corpus of Early Medieval Inscribed Stones and Stone Sculptures in Wales*, 3 vols. (Cardiff: University of Wales Press, 2007–13), 3:130, 3:384.

[130] David Wilson, *The Vikings in the Isle of Man* (Aarhus: Aarhus University Press, 2008), 38–46.

[131] Philip M. C. Kermode, *Manx Crosses* (1907; Dundee: Pink-

foot, 1994); Graham-Campbell, *Viking Art*, 22; Dirk H. Steinforth, "Early Vikings in the Isles of Man: Old Paradigms and New Perspectives," *Viking and Medieval Scandinavia* 11 (2015): 203–29; Jesch, *The Viking Diaspora*, 171.

132 James Graham-Campbell, *Vikingenes Verden* (Oslo: Tiden Norsk, 1980), 72. www.manxdna.co.uk.

133 *Diplomatarium Norvegicum*, 23 vols. to date with multiple parts (Oslo [Christiania]: Malling, 1849-), vol. 8 (pt. 1), November 30, 1154.

134 Val E. Turner and Ian A. Simpson, "Landscapes of Settlement: Inheritance and Sustainability in Shetland's Viking Farms," in *Shetland and the Viking World: Papers from the Seventeenth Viking Congress, Lerwick*, ed. Val E. Turner, Olwyn A. Owen, and Doreen J. Waugh (Lerwick: Shetland Heritage, 2016), 25–30.

135 Brian Smith, "The Picts and the Martyrs or Did Vikings Kill the Native Population of Orkney and Shetland?," *Northern Studies* 36 (2001): 7–32; Jessica Bäcklund, "The Norse in Orkney. An Archaeological and Social Antrhopological Study of the Norse Settlement Process and the Relationship between the Norse and the Picts" (PhD diss., University of Edinburgh, 2001).

136 Andrew Jennings and Arne Kruse, "An Ethnic Enigma—Norse, Pict and Gael in the Western Isles," in *Viking and Norse in the North Atlantic: Select Papers from the Proceedings of the Fourteenth Viking Congress Tórshavn, 19–30 July 2001*, ed. Andras Mortensen and Símun V. Arge (Tórshavn: Føroya, 2005), 284–96.

137 Oliver J. T. Harris et al., "Assembling Places and Persons: A Tenth-Century Viking Boat Burial from Swordle Bay on the Ardnamurchan Peninsula, Western Scotland," *Antiquity* 91, no. 355 (2017), pp. 191–206. http://dx.doi.org/10.15184/aqy.2016.222.

138 Jesch, *The Viking Diaspora*, 171–72.

139 Agnar Helgason et al., "Mt-DNA and the Origin of Icelanders: Deciphering Signals of Recent Population History," *American Journal of Human Genetics* 66 (2000): 999–1016; Agnar Helgason et al., "MtDNA and the Islands of the North Atlantic: Estimating the Proportions of Norse and Gaelic Ancestry," *American Journal of Human Genetics* 68 (2001): 723–37; Stephen H. Harrison, "'Warrior Graves'? The Weapon Burial Rite in Viking Age Britain and Ireland," in *Maritime Societies of the Viking and Medieval World*, ed. James H Barrett and Sarah Jane Gibbon (Leeds: Maney, 2015), 299–319.

140 Our translation, after that from *Landnåmabok* by Jan Ragnar Hagland (Stavanger: Erling Skjalgssonselskapet, 2002), 36.

141 Kevin J. Edwards, E. Erlendsson, and J. E. Schofield, "Is there

a Norse 'footprint' in North Atlantic pollen records," in *Viking Settlements and Society: Papers from the Sixteenth Viking Congress, Reykjavík and Reykholt, 16–23 August 2009*, ed. Svavar Sigmundsson et al. (Reykjavík: Hið íslenska fornleifafélag / University of Iceland Press, 2011), 65–82.

[142] Bjørn Myhre, Bjarne Stoklund, and Per Gjærder, eds., *Vestnordisk byggeskikk gjennom to tusen år*, Ams Skrifter 7 (Stavanger: Arkeologisk Museum, 1982).

[143] J. E. Schofield and Kevin J. Edwards, "Peat and People in Greenland," in *Shetland and the Viking World: Papers from the Seventeenth Viking Congress, Lerwick*, ed. Val E. Turner, Olwyn A. Owen, and Doreen J. Waugh (Lerwick: Shetland Heritage, 2016), 91–96.

[144] Kevin J. Edwards and Douglas B. Borthwick, "Peaceful Wars and Scientific Invaders: Irishmen, Vikings and Palynological Evidence for the Earliest Settlement of the Faroe Islands," in *The Viking Age. Ireland and the West*, ed. Sheehan and Ó Corráin, 66–79; Mike J. Church et al., "The Vikings Were Not the First Colonizers of the Faroe Islands," *Quaternary Science Reviews* 77 (2013): 228–32.

[145] Steffen Stummann Hansen, "Toftanes. A Viking Age Farmstead in the Faroe Islands," *Acta Archaeologica* 84, no. 1 (2013): 5–239.

[146] Steffen Stummann Hansen and John Sheehan, "The Leirvik 'Bøhústoftin' and the Early Christianity of the Faroe Islands, and Beyond," *Archaeologica Islandica* 5 (2006): 27–54; Símun V. Arge, "Christianity, Churches and Medieval Kirkjubøur—Contacts and Influences in the Faroe Islands," in *Medieval Archaeology in Scandinavia and Beyond: History, Trends and Tomorrow. Proceedings of a Conference to Celebrate 40 years of Medieval Archaeology at Aarhus University, 26–27 October 2011*, ed. Mette Svart Kristensen, Else Roesdahl, and James Graham-Campbell (Aarhus: Aarhus University Press, 2015), 235–56.

[147] Simun V. Arge, Guðrún Sveinbjarnardóttir, Kevin J. Edwards, and Paul C. Buckland, "Viking and Medieval Settlement in the Faroes: People, Place and Environment," *Human Ecology* 33, no. 5 (October 2005): 597–620.

[148] Orri Vésteinsson and Thomas H. McGovern, "The Peopling of Iceland," *Norwegian Archaeological Review* 45, no. 2 (2012): 206–18, and see the responses.

[149] Helgason et al., "Mt-DNA and the Origin of Icelanders," and Helgason et al., "MtDNA and the Islands of the North Atlantic"; Steinunn Kristjánsdóttir, "The Vikings as a Diaspora. Cultural

and Religious Identities in Early Medieval Iceland," in *Viking Settlements and Viking Society. Papers from the Proceedings of the 16th Viking Congress, Reykjavík and Reykholt, 16-23 August 2009*, ed. Svavar Sigmundsson (Reykjavík: Hid Islenzka Fornleifafélag / University of Iceland Press, 2011), 422-36.

[150] S. Sunna Ebenesersdóttir et al., "Supplementary Materials. Ancient Genomes from Iceland Reveal the Making of a Human Population," *Science* 360 (2018): 1-58.

[151] Thóra Pétursdóttir, "Icelandic Viking Age Graves: Lack in Material—Lack of Interpretation?," *Archaeologia Islandica* 7 (2009): 22-40; Steinunn Kristjánsdóttir, "The Vikings as a Diaspora"; Adolf Fridriksson and Orri Vésteinsson, "Landscapes of Burial: Contrasting the Pagan and Christian Paradigms of Burial in Viking Age and Medieval Iceland," *Archaeologia Islandica* 9 (2011): 50-64.

[152] Kevin J. Edwards, J. E. Schofield, R. Craigie, "Norse landscape impacts: Northern Isles versus the North Atlantic islands," in *Shetland and the Viking World: Papers from the Seventeenth Viking Congress, Lerwick*, ed. Val E. Turner, Olwyn A. Owen, and Doreen J. Waugh (Lerwick: Shetland Heritage, 2016), 77-84.

[153] David Zori et al., "Feasting in Viking Age Iceland: Sustainig a Chiefly Political Economy in a Marginal Environment," *Antiquity* 87 (2013): 150-65; Scott Riddell et al., "Cereal Cultivation as a Correlate of High Social Status in Medieval Iceland," *Vegetation History and Archaeobotany* (2017): 150-65.

[154] Thomas H. McGovern et al., "Landscape of Settlement in Northern Iceland: Historical Ecology of Human Impact and Climate Fluctuation on the Millennial Scale," *American Anthropologist* 109, no. 1 (2007): 27-51.

[155] Steinunn Kristjánsdóttir, *The Awakening of Christianity in Iceland : Discovery of a Timber Church and Graveyard at Þórarinsstaðir in Seyðisfjörður*, Gotarc Series B. Gothenburg Archaeological Theses 31, 2 vols. (Gothenburg: Göteborgs universitet, 2004); Orri Vésteinsson, "The Formative Phase of the Icelandic Church Ca. 990-1240 AD," in *Church Centres: Church Centres in Iceland from the 11th to the 13th Century and Their Parallels in Other Countries*, ed. Thorláksson Helgi (Reykholt: Snorrastofa, 2005), 6-7.

[156] A. J. Dugmore et al., "The Norse landnám on the North Atlantic islands: an environmental impact assessment," *Polar Record* 41 (2005): 21-37.

[157] Thomas H. McGovern, "Cows, harp seals, and churchbells: adaptation and extinction in Norse Greenland," *Human Ecology* 8 (1980): 245-75.

[158] Svend Erik Albrethsen and Jette Arneborg, *Norse Ruins of the Southern Paamiut and Ivittuut Region*, Danish Polar Center Publication 13 (Copenhagen: SILA—Greenland Research Centre, National Museum of Denmark, 2004); Kevin J. Edwards et al., "Towards a First Chronology for the Middle Settlement of Norse Greenland: 14C and Related Studies of Animal Bone and Environmental Material," *Radiocarbon* 55, no. 1 (2013): 1–17.

[159] Niels Lynnerup, "Endperiod Demographics of the Greenland Norse," *Journal of the North Atlantic* Special Volume 7 (2014): 18–24.

[160] Kevin J. Edwards, and J. E. Schofield, "Investigation of proposed Norse irrigation channels and dams at Garðar/Igaliku, Greenland," *Water History* 5 (2013): 71–92.

[161] W. P. Adderley, and I. A. Simpson, "Soils and palaeo-climate based evidence for irrigation requirements in Norse Greenland," *Journal of Archaeological Science* 33 (2006): 1666–79; P. C. Buckland, Kevin J. Edwards, E. Panagiotakopulu, and J. E. Schofield, "Palaeoecological Evidence for Manuring and Irrigation at Garðar (Igaliku), Norse Eastern Settlement, Greenland," *The Holocene* 19 (2009): 105–16.

[162] Jette Arneborg, Niels Lynnerup, and Jan Heinemeier, "Human Diet and Subsistence Patterns in Norse Greenland AD *c.* 980–AD *c.* 1450: Archaeological Interpretations," *Journal of the North Atlantic* Special Volume 3 (2012): 119–33.

[163] Karin M. Frei et al., "Was it for walrus? Viking Age settlement and medieval walrus ivory trade in Iceland and Greenland," *World Archaeology* 47, no. 3 (2015): 439–66.

[164] Bastiaan Star et al., "Ancient DNA reveals the chronology of walrus ivory trade from Norse Greenland. *Proceedings of the Royal Society of London B.: Biological Sciences* 285, no. 1884 (2018): 9152–57 and online: http://dx.doi.org/10.1098/rspb.2018.0978.

[165] Mogens Skaaning Høegsberg, "Continuity and Change: The Dwellings of the Greenland Norse," *Journal of the North Atlantic* Special Volume 2 (2009): 82–101.

[166] Anne Stine Ingstad, et al., *The Discovery of a Norse Settlement in America. Excavations at L'Anse aux Meadows, Newfoundland 1961-1968* (Oslo: Universitetsforlaget, 1977), vol. 1 of a two-volume set.

[167] Birgitta Wallace, "L'Anse aux Meadows, Leif Eriksson's Home in Vinland," *Journal of the North Atlantic* Special Volume 2 (2009): 114–25.

[168] Wallace, "L'Anse aux Meadows."

Chapter 4

The Viking Phenomenon

In the preceding pages, the Viking phenomenon, in terms of events lasting up to the mid-eleventh century, has been presented in a highly summarized and selective form. The "who," "when," and "where" relating to that astonishing group have been recounted, and various antecedent conditions have been mentioned. The key question of "why" has not been developed, so let us now introduce a brief examination of this topic as a prelude to itemizing some factors which we consider to be significant, or of interest, to the Viking experience, and this is followed by an examination of the Viking legacy.

Why Did the Vikings Occur?

In a thoughtful summary review of the causes behind the advent of the Vikings, James Barrett listed the following aspects that he went on to assess in turn:[169]

- *Technological determinism*: the Vikings were renowned for their sea power and seamanship, but there is no reason why this could not have happened earlier given prevailing expertise.

- *Environmental determinism*: the Medieval Warm Period, whatever its reality and geographical limits, meant that warm ocean temperatures and minimal sea-ice conditions acted as permissive factors, though probably not causal ones.

- *Demographic determinism*: evidence for population pressures is probably piecemeal and nebulous, whereas the militarization of pre-Christian Scandinavia associated with state formation might favour female infanticide and the need to acquire bride-price or a dowry.

- *Economic determinism*: raiding opportunities on monasteries and proto-urban *wics* (that is, a "gold-rush mentality," "silver fever") may have been irresistible, especially if Arabic silver shortages occurred, and slave-trading was always an attraction.

- *Political determinism*: power through wealth, land acquisition, and reputation.

- *Ideological determinism*: intertwined aspects of religion, militarism, honour, fatalism, and peer pressure.

By variously accepting or rejecting these potential causal factors, Barrett assembled a portmanteau explanation which might be stated as: bands of young men seeking bride-wealth, joined by powerful social superiors, and imbued with a sense of fatalism, created a desire for wealth to fuel ambitions within and beyond Scandinavia.

There is not necessarily much to object to in Barrett's conclusion and many of these elements are a combination of push and pull factors. It might be asked if there was not simply an aspect of migration akin to that seen in later European migrations to North America or Australasia, or African and Near Eastern migrations to Europe—people searching for a better life, economically and socially, pursued according to the mores of their times, which in the Viking era often meant ruthlessly. Once the Viking momentum was established, it becomes perhaps as much about participating in what had become an almost fashionable activity—there may not always have been an expectation of riches and position (or not for rank and file participants), and with a fair wind metaphorically and in reality, people might have been able to return from whence they came. This is not a prosaic explanation, but one which might cover the majority of migrants even if the organization was mainly in the hands of more ambitious and scheming individuals.

The Viking Experience

What are the significant factors and issues which might be considered to have typified the Viking experience? This volume is witness to such aspects. Arising from what we have shown above are those "angles" which are intriguing or worthy of comment and further consideration and exploration, including:

- Many aspects of Viking-like activity are to be found prior to the Viking Age; it is a moot point whether the start of the "Viking Age" should be altered from 800 to ca. 700.

- Eastern Europe has produced a much higher number of Viking artefacts than is generally realised.

- In spite of their probably small size in terms of population, the Vikings were able to control larger populations and over great distances through the use of terror and power.

- Although displaying aspects of conformity, the Vikings were also a disparate set of communities, especially within Scandinavia.

- The Vikings raided within Scandinavia as well as beyond its shores.

- The relationship, spatial and temporal, between the Vikings and urbanization is not definitively proven, although there is some clear overlap.

- More men than women migrated, but gender roles were diverse and it is clear that some women at least took on major societal roles.

- In the North Atlantic area, we do not observe typical Viking activities. The area was essentially empty when the Norse arrived and the priority was to fashion an economy and society which enabled life to endure in alien and extreme landscapes.

- With the accrued power of the Vikings, it might be imagined that the North Atlantic adventure was being driven by a great pulsating economic, political, and military regime. It was, however, an essentially fragmented, disorganized power (for instance, the geographical areas of the Danelaw waxed and waned and there were internal factions, while Ireland came to be "lost"); and, arguably, the North Atlantic islands were never *that* important.Apart from anything else, the spread across the North Atlantic was not inevitable—the resources within Europe were probably enough. Was the North Atlantic a release valve—the path of least resistance in the face of European resistance?

- Science is adding precision to, and altering perceptions of, views of Viking life. This applies especially to human and animal genetics, but also to isotopes and a suite of environmentally-related approaches (e.g., radiocarbon-dating, tephrochronology, dendroprovenancing, palaeo-environmental analyses).

What Stopped the Vikings?

The Battle of Hastings in 1066 was the result of a new era—a conflict between kings rather than raiding Vikings. Although this event has been posited as the end of the Viking Age, it might be said that there were other contributory factors, such as:

- The Vikings lacked academic skills, such as numeracy and literacy, thwarting a higher level of organization.

- Ship technology and re-armament improved in areas of the Viking diaspora, enabling indigenous communities to resist attacks and regain control.

- Religious and cultural differences made it difficult for people in Scandinavia to interact with those from outside the area, even with their own converted relatives in the diaspora. Vikings violated religious sites, and Christians were discouraged from mixing with non-believers. This made it difficult for Scandinavian towns to function as international centres and steps were taken to change the situation. The Christians established the archbishopric of Hamburg–Bremen in 831–845, while Scandinavian leaders saw that Christianity could be helpful in seeking power, with, for instance, the Church's ideology of supporting a ruling hierarchy and providing academic skills in writing, keeping accounts, legislation, taxation, art and architecture. The Scandinavian elite converted and persuaded or forced their followers and charges to do the same. This resulted in the emergence of Christian monarchies in Scandinavia from around 1000. The Scandinavians were effectively Europeanized and Viking raids stopped.

The Viking Legacy

Even if the Scandinavians stopped raiding, their leaders did not stop fighting. The kings or petty kings continued to fight each other, within Scandinavia or beyond, as at Hastings, or as crusaders they fought alongside their foreign counterparts in the name of the Church.

In alliance with the Church, the Norse maintained a grip on some of their target areas. When an archbishopric was established in Nidaros in 1153, Iceland, Greenland, the Faroe Islands, the Hebrides, Orkney and Shetland, and the Isle of Man were placed under Norse control. Since then, and in times of relative peace, the Vikings have held a fascination within and outwith Scandinavia. Medieval authors like Snorri Sturlusson wrote the history of Viking kings, while pre-Christian religion and motifs on churches relate to earlier beliefs (stave churches in Norway are well known for their dragons and other symbols; Figure 31). Eighteenth- and nineteenth-century Scandinavian romanticism in art, literature, and history was imbued with a Viking essence and today there is no shortage of Viking re-enactment groups, popular books, films, and television series, nor any lack of themed tourism enterprises and "Viking trails" (Figure 32).

The Viking Age was one of the most dynamic periods in Scandinavian history, and it continues to attract extensive

Figure 31. The richly decorated Borgund stave church,
in Sogn, Norway.

Figure 32. Roadside tourist sign, New foundland, Canada.

scholarly attention. Research, teaching, and symposia such as the quasi-exclusive four-yearly Viking Congress (since 1950), or more open meetings such as the three-yearly Saga Conferences (since 1971), act as foci and catalysts for Viking study.

Viking symbols and ideology have also been appropriated by ultra-conservative political movements—from the Nazis through to neo-fascists in Europe and North America. Neo-Nazis are still using a Thor's hammer as a symbol while Anders Behring Breivik, a racist mass murderer fighting for an extreme Christian mono-cultural society, killed seventy-seven people in Norway in 2011 and was described as a "Viking" by supporters.

Conquest and migration did not start, nor end, with the Vikings. As a major part of the history of a substantial portion of the Northern Hemisphere, and as a culture which still features in the popular imagination, the Vikings are worthy of attention. Discovering more about them helps us to understand our history and its trajectory.

Notes

169 James H. Barrett. "What Caused the Viking Age?," *Antiquity* 82, no. 317 (September 2008): 671–85; James H. Barrett, "Rounding Up the Usual Suspects: Causation and the Viking Age Diaspora," in *The Global Origins and Development of Seafaring*, ed. Atholl Anderson, James H. Barrett, and Katherine V. Boyle (Cambridge: McDonald Institute for Archaeological Research, University of Cambridge, 2010), 289–302.

Further Reading

This list combines books that are popular as well as those of more specialist appeal.

Ahola, Joonas, and Frog, eds. *Fibula, Fabula, Fact. The Viking Age in Finland*. Studia Fennica Historica 18, Helsinki: Finnish Literature Society, 2014.
> An interdisciplinary study on Finland discussing cultural heritage relevant to Viking Age history.

Androshchuk, Fedir. *Vikings in the East. Essays on Contact Along the Road to Byzantium (800–1100)*. Studia Byzantina Upsaliensia 14. Uppsala: Uppsala Universitet, 2013

Barrett, James H., ed. *Contact, Continuity, and Collapse: The Norse Colonization of the North Atlantic*. Turnhout: Brepols, 2003.
> A collection of papers investigating the Norse colonization of the North Atlantic region, including Viking expansion in Arctic Norway and the medieval Scandinavian exploration of North America.

Brink, Stefan, ed. *The Viking World*. In collaboration with Neil Price. London: Routledge, 2008.
> A comprehensive volume with articles on key issues of the Viking world.

Byock, Jesse L. *Viking Age Iceland*. New edn. London: Penguin, 2001.
> An in-depth, readable assessment of Viking Age society in Iceland with observations on ethnography, the law, archaeology, and history.

Christiansen, Eric. *The Norsemen in the Viking Age*. Peoples of Europe. Oxford: Blackwell, 2006.

> An intriguing book which meshes archaeology, literature and considerations of Viking society, politics, war, and work.

Christys, Ann. *Vikings in the South: Voyages to Iberia and the Mediterranean*. Studies in Early Medieval History. London: Bloomsbury, 2015.

Duczko, Wladyslaw. *Viking Rus: Studies on the Presence of Scandinavians in Eastern Europe*. The Northern World 12. Leiden: Brill, 2004.

Edwards, Kevin J. "On the Windy Edge of Nothing: Vikings in the North Atlantic World—Ecological and Social Journeys." The 2012 Rhind Lectures, Society of Antiquaries of Scotland. April 13–15, 2012. 7 videos. https://www.youtube.com/watch?v=YQB0kHuCk8Y&list=PLomxm-mDt-nnJ8JjuT2YXGmMoASc6bYgtb

> Well-illustrated audio and PowerPoint videos of these lectures, with their emphasis upon Norse settlement, landscape, and environment in the North Atlantic world.

Fitzhugh, William W., and Elisabeth I. Ward, eds. *Vikings: The North Atlantic Saga*. Washington, DC: Smithsonian Institution Press, 2000.

> A lavishly illustrated tome dealing concisely with many aspects of Viking life and colonization from Europe across the Atlantic to North America and including much relevant material on archaeology, history, literature, and science.

Foote, Peter G., and David M. Wilson. *The Viking Achievement: The Society and Culture of Early Medieval Scandinavia*. London: Sidgwick & Jackson, 1970.

> A classic eminently readable book on the Viking Age, particularly strong on society and the law and many other topics besides.

Graham-Campbell, James. *Viking Art*. World of Art. London: Thames & Hudson, 2013.

> A well-illustrated overview of Scandinavian art—one of the characteristics of the Viking Age.

Jesch, Judith. *The Viking Diaspora*. The Medieval World. London: Routledge, 2015.

> A focus on the movements of people in the Viking world and their shared heritage and culture, with due consideration of family, gender, religion, and identity.

Mägi, Marika, *In Austrvegr: The Role of the Eastern Baltic in the Viking Age. Communication Across the Baltic Sea*. The Northern World 84. Leiden: Brill, 2018.

Magnusson, Magnus. *The Vikings*. Stroud: Tempus, 2003.

> An exceptionally readable historical narrative of the Vikings.

Munch, Gerd Stamsø, Olav Sverre Johansen, and Else Roesdahl, eds. *Borg in Lofoten: A Chieftain's Farm in North Norway*. Arkeologisk Skriftserie 1. Trondheim: Tapir, 2003.

> Based on excavations, this book presents one of the most important Viking Age farms in Norway featuring the longest house in Viking Age Scandinavia.

Page, Raymond I. *Chronicles of the Vikings: Records, Memorials and Myths*. London: British Museum, 1995.

> A book about Vikings and how they viewed themselves based on written accounts.

Price, Neil S. *The Viking Way: Religion and War in Late Iron Age Scandinavia*. Aun 31. Uppsala: Department of Archaeology and Ancient History, University of Uppsala, 2002.

> A fascinating study of Norse paganism in Scandinavia with a focus on religion, mythology, shamanism, magic, and the mind.

Richards, Julian D. *Viking Age England*. Stroud: History Press, 2012.

> A comprehensive book on Viking Age England.

Roesdahl, Else. *The Vikings*, trans. by Susan Margeson and Kirsten Williams. 3rd ed. London: Penguin, 2016.

> A comprehensive and concise overview of the Vikings.

Roesdahl, Else, Søren M. Sindbæk, and Anne Pedersen, eds. *Aggersborg i vikingetiden: bebyggelsen og borgen*, Jysk Arkæologisk Selskabs skrifter 81. Højbjerg: Jysk Arkæologisk Selskab, 2014.

> A discussion of Aggersborg, the largest of the Danish Viking ring-forts in the context of similar monuments.

Sawyer, Peter, ed. *The Oxford Illustrated History of the Vikings*. Oxford: Oxford University Press, 2001.

> A collection of well-illustrated essays on the Viking homelands and the diaspora.

Seaver, Kirsten A. *The Last Vikings. The Epic Story of the Great Norse Voyages*. London: I. B. Tauris, 2010.

> A readable and critical analysis of the characters, history, archaeology, and politics surrounding the Norse occupation of Greenland and its relationship to key participants in Europe and North America.

Schietzel, Kurt, et al. *Spurensuche Haithabu: archäologische Spurensuche in der frühmittelalterlichen Ansiedlung Haithabu. Dokumentation und Chronik 1963–2013*. Neumünster: Wachholtz, 2014.

> A comprehensive, lavishly illustrated presentation of knowledge concerning the Viking town of Haithabu.

Steinsland, Gro. *Norrøn religion: myter, riter, samfunn*. Oslo: Pax, 2005.

> A scholarly text on Old Norse religion, based mainly on written sources.

Svanberg, Fredrik. *Decolonizing the Viking Age*. 2 vols. Acta Archaeologica Lundensia 24 and 43. Lund: Almqvist & Wiksell International, 2003.

> A doctoral thesis providing a good overview of Viking Age material in south-east Scandinavia, 800–1000, analysed from a postcolonial perspective and focusing on local variations.

Valante, Mary A. *The Vikings in Ireland: Settlement, Trade and Urbanization*. Dublin: Four Courts, 2008.

> A good overview of Viking Age Ireland from a historian's perspective.